**NEW DIRECTIONS
FOR TEACHING AND
LEARNING**

Number 6 • 1981

NEW DIRECTIONS FOR TEACHING AND LEARNING

A Quarterly Sourcebook
Kenneth E. Eble, John F. Noonan, Editors-in-Chief

Number 6, 1981

Liberal Learning and Careers

Charles S. Green III
Richard G. Salem
Editors

Jossey-Bass Inc., Publishers
San Francisco • Washington • London

LIBERAL LEARNING AND CAREERS
New Directions for Teaching and Learning
Number 6, 1981
Charles S. Green III, Richard G. Salem, Editors

Copyright © 1981 by Jossey-Bass Inc., Publishers
and
Jossey-Bass Limited

New Directions for Teaching and Learning is published quarterly
by Jossey-Bass Inc., Publishers. Subscriptions are available
at the regular rate for institutions, libraries, and agencies
of $30 for one year. Individuals may subscribe at the special
professional rate of $18 for one year.

Correspondence:
Subscriptions, single-issue orders, change of address notices,
undelivered copies, and other correspondence should be sent to
New Directions Subscriptions, Jossey-Bass Inc., Publishers,
433 California Street, San Francisco, California 94104.

Editorial correspondence should be sent to the Editors-in-Chief,
Kenneth E. Eble or John F. Noonan, Center for Improving
Teaching Effectiveness, Virginia Commonwealth University,
Richmond, Virginia 23284.

Library of Congress Catalogue Card Number LC 81-81859
International Standard Serial Number ISSN 0271-0633
International Standard Book Number ISBN 87589-867-X

Cover design by Willi Baum
Manufactured in the United States of America

Contents

vi

Editors' Notes

Retrenchment may well be the burning issue of the 1980s for many if not most colleges and universities. However, with much less fanfare, retrenchment had already become an issue for most liberal arts disciplines by the middle of the 1970s. Whereas ten years ago enrollments in the liberal arts disciplines were booming despite such "reforms" of the 1960s as the elimination of foreign language requirements, now the very existence of liberal learning is threatened by changing enrollment patterns. For example, between 1972-73 and 1978-79, the number of bachelor's degrees awarded by the entire University of Wisconsin System dropped 46 percent in arts and letters and 32 percent in the social sciences, but increased 35 percent in both business management and public services (University of Wisconsin System, 1979). Nationwide, the number of bachelor's degrees awarded in sociology peaked at 36,000 in 1973; by 1979 the number had declined 40 percent to 22,000 (U.S. National Center for Education Statistics, 1980). In 1969, "Religious Ideas in Literature" was the most popular course at Princeton University; now the most popular course is "The Structure and Functioning of the National Economy" (Associated Press, 1979). It should be no news to any academician that such changes characterize virtually every college and university (Middleton, 1979; Riesman, 1978). In summary, during the 1970s, despite continued high *total* college and university enrollment, enrollments *within* colleges and universities shifted in massive proportions from the liberal arts to such vocational programs as engineer-

The editors wish to acknowledge those who have given their encouragement and support during the creation of this book: Everett Fulton, William Greer, Hadley Klug, Lanny Neider, Anton Mueller, Robert Sweet, Mathew Zachariah, at the University of Wisconsin-Whitewater; Theodore Argiris, president, Alpha-Cast Inc.; Robert Bierstedt, University of Virginia; Frederic Campbell, University of Washington; Emily Dunn Dale, Illinois Wesleyan University; Kenneth Eble, University of Utah; Joseph and Joann Elder, University of Wisconsin-Madison; David Kamens, Northern Illinois University; Rita Kirschstein, SUNY College at Buffalo; William Mayrl, University of Wisconsin-Milwaukee; Earl Ramsey, University of Arkansas-Little Rock; David Riesman, Harvard University; Martin Trow, University of California-Berkeley; Sister Marlene Weber, Viterbo College. Our task would have been far more difficult without the secretarial and administrative expertise of Clarice Piper.

ing, social welfare, health services, business administration, and criminal justice. This volume has two purposes: to trace the reasons for this massive enrollment shift and to assess the kinds of responses that the liberal arts can and should make to this shift.

The lead chapter by Edgar Litt is a highly provocative analysis of the reasons behind the vocationalization of American colleges and universities, particularly the public ones. Litt's thesis is that governmental regulatory and budgetary decisions made in the name of accountability, social equity, and efficiency are forcing higher education to increase the coordination of research, course offerings, and curricula not only with student preferences but also with the job market for highly specialized managerial and technical skills. Lewis Solmon's companion chapter reports the findings from large-scale, longitudinal surveys of the employment experiences of two cohorts of entering college freshmen. One of the more important of Solmon's findings is that choice of major field has a significant impact on both earnings and perceived underemployment. Arts, humanities, and social science majors not only earn less than those majoring in engineering, business, and other vocational fields but also are more likely to feel underemployed. Since students' choices of major field are affected by their perceptions of job market opportunities, the massive enrollment shifts of the 1970s are partly explainable in terms of the different job opportunities made available to college graduates with different major fields of study.

But why are job opportunities better for those choosing vocational majors than for those choosing liberal arts majors? Solmon notes that "engineers, for example, are just assumed [by employers] to be brighter than English majors." The issue of the correctness of this assumption need not detain us here because it is discussed in greater detail in several of the chapters in this volume. But one thing is certain: Hiring decisions based on such an assumption create a self-fulfilling prophecy. If no English majors are hired, no evidence to refute the assumption is ever encountered. Unfortunately, most of the responses to declining enrollments in the liberal arts have failed to challenge the assumption directly.

Some campuses, most notably Harvard, have responded by reversing many of the curricular changes made in the 1960s by introducing required courses in math, English, and foreign languages, reintroducing distribution requirements, and developing minimum standards of competency. While these changes have served to increase enrollments in introductory-level courses on many campuses, it is significant that these changes have failed to increase the number of students majoring in the liberal arts. In short, the trend toward vocationalism appears to be a fundamental one, irreversible by such expedients as increasing the number of required courses in the liberal arts.

There are other responses being made to declining enrollments. Two of these are especially troubling. One involves diluting major requirements and making courses less difficult (Hansen, Stivers, and Francis, 1976; Riesman, 1978). The other response, distinguishable from but related to the first, involves introducing more "practical" and "relevant" courses. For example, English departments across the country have been introducing or expanding existing offerings in technical writing and "business English" to compensate for declining enrollments in literature courses. In sociology there has been a proliferation of courses in criminology and social welfare methods (Green and others, 1980). The growth of enrollment in such courses has been so phenomenal that it has triggered the splitting of existing sociology departments as well as stimulating the creation of wholly new departments or programs. The irony, if not the lesson, of such developments is obvious. The editors and, we suspect, the other contributors to this volume think these last two responses deserve wholehearted rejection by the liberal arts disciplines. First, they are not really practical responses. Rather, they represent "crackpot realism," a term coined by the sociologist C. Wright Mills to describe American public-policy decisions as diverse as hiring more police to deal with rising crime rates, building fallout shelters in basements, and destroying villages in order to save them. If it is true that most nonacademic employers do not understand what the liberal arts are or what liberal arts graduates can do, then it seems the height of folly to adapt the curriculum to their misunderstanding. Since such misunderstanding is likely to be caused by the employer's own lack of liberal education and contact with employees educated in the liberal arts, the best strategy is to change the employer's knowledge and attitudes rather than curricula. Such a strategy of subversion—and of enlightenment—can be effected most quickly by placing more liberal arts majors in internships and in regular employment with nonacademic employers (Brown and Allen, 1979). Ultimately, however, what is done in the classroom *now* to educate *future* employers is the greatest force for change.

There is a second and even more fundamental basis for challenging such responses as diluting major requirements and making courses easier, more relevant, and practical. These types of responses are intellectually dishonest. In the area of criminology, for example, the intellectual quality of many of the new courses and programs has been severely criticized by the National Advisory Commission on Higher Education for Police Officers (Sherman, 1978). In a world of intellectual ferment and vast social, economic, and political change, it is intellectually dishonest not to tell students that any course that pretends to be relevant or practical today will be obsolete and irrelevant within five to ten years (Ebersole, 1979). Furthermore, it is intellectually dishonest to pretend that vocationalizing the curriculum as a whole will do anything but sustain those values the liberal arts have traditionally disdained. We must convey to our students that a liberal arts education is, ideally, a liberating experience—and that by liberation we mean above all else liberation from the pressure to be relevant and practical.

However, we also think it is irresponsible for academicians to ignore the present, for the career concerns of undergraduate students are real, compelling, and legitimate (Coleman, 1972; Dayton, 1979; Munschauer, 1979; Terry, 1979). Is there any way to respond to their concerns without compromising intellectual integrity? We believe there is.

First, it is imperative that the liberal arts extricate themselves from the pessimism and malaise that have prevailed since the mid-1960s (Ackerman, 1969). Vocational training in applied science, engineering, and administration has gained favor over the liberal arts because it has seemed self-evident even in academia that only those so trained could solve serious contemporary problems (Dieter, 1980). But it can be argued just as plausibly that those problems were *created* by persons trained in applied science, engineering, and administration. For were they not the ones who brought us the gas-guzzling car, Love Canal and other "better things for better living through chemistry," Three Mile Island, acid rain and oil spills, even Watergate? Vocationally trained persons may know how to do things, but they do not have the depth of historical vision, the capacity for envisioning the future, or the ethical sensitivities and aesthetic sensibilities to know why certain things should be done—and why certain other things should *not* be done. Only liberal learning can provide such wisdom, however imperfect that wisdom must inevitably be. That this wisdom is of inestimable value is the message we must convey to the general public. The next four chapters provide us with the essential components of this message.

Donald Honicky argues that the long-range needs of business require people with broad, general education rather than narrow, vocational training in business or engineering. He further argues for closer relations between business and higher education. In so doing he describes a number of college-relations programs that have proved mutually beneficial to the business and colleges or universities involved.

Alberta Arthurs outlines the various programs of a small, private, liberal arts college, of which she is president, that were developed to respond to the career concerns of its students. She shows how the study of a work of English literature seemingly unrelated to the world of business, Sir Thomas Malory's *Morte d'Arthur*, actually provides cognitive skills crucial to the long-run needs of business—and of the nation as a whole. The study of Malory's work provides students with insights into human motivations and moral issues that transcend the particularities of time and place, requires students to analyze the workings of institutions and an individual's role in them, and develops in students a sense of tragedy and of the seductiveness of the vision of perfection.

Clinton Adam's chapter traces the erratic historical process by which the arts have begun to be integrated into the general education curriculum. He provides the compelling argument that artistic visions, like theories in the natural and social sciences, are essential for the vitality, perhaps even the survival, of our civilization. Adams makes the further observation that despite the recent growth of the arts as a component in general education, most Americans remain aesthetically illiterate. The consequences of that illiteracy are painfully evident in the recent debates over the introduction of mobile MX missile sites and over strip mining for coal and oil shale in the American West. These debates have focused on economic issues to the exclusion of aesthetic ones (Ivins, 1980). That we are more literate in economics than in aesthetics bodes ill for our civilization for, as one wag noted, an economist is someone who knows the price of everything but the value of nothing.

Vivian Gordon's chapter is concerned with black studies. She traces the emergence of black studies programs on white campuses through the turmoil and quest for relevance of the 1960s and early 1970s, noting the reasons for the weaknesses and failures of those programs. In discussing the promise of black studies, she makes the perceptive observation that all the liberal arts disciplines that broke away from the parent discipline, philosophy, faced the same enormous difficulties black studies does in defining its boundaries and establishing its legitimacy. Gordon further notes that black studies has a firm intellectual foundation in the tradition of theory and research established by such early black scholars as W.E.B. DuBois, E. Franklin Frazier, and John Hope Franklin. Her chapter concludes with a proposal for a new black studies curriculum that is far more coherent and intellectually demanding than its predecessors.

Thus, these four chapters provide the components for an important message that we must convey to the public: that liberal learning is intrinsically valuable to every sector of the nation. Presumably, our credibility in communicating that message to the public can be preserved only if we ourselves are so convinced of the validity of that message that we refuse to compromise on either the traditional content or the standards of liberal learning. The next four chapters are concerned with a variety of responses that liberal arts disciplines can include in their traditional curricula without compromising either course content or standards.

Geoffrey Marshall's chapter discusses recent innovative trends in the curricula of the liberal arts and humanities, trends Marshall discerns from his analysis of the grant applications submitted to the National Endowment for the Humanities. While the structure and content of the major have remained the same, there have been significant changes made in the role of the humanities in general education and in the education of non-majors. Marshall then turns to the difficult decade of the 1980s, discussing the necessity for faculty planning for the future if the humanities are to survive, let alone thrive. He suggests innovation in three areas: programs for the general public, improved teaching at the elementary and secondary level, and greater collaboration between the humanities and business.

The chapter by Charles Green and others describes a four-part program implemented by a sociology department to cope with the career concerns of its students. A handbook for actual and prospective sociology majors both defines sociology as a discipline and provides information on career opportunities. The second part of the program involves the combination of intensive career counseling with academic advising, while the third part is a closely supervised internship. The fourth part is a seminar in career development, which provides students with information on graduate education and with job-seeking skills, such as interviewing and resume writing.

In the next chapter James Parins reviews the evolution of a small, private, liberal arts college into a large, urban, public university. In the course of that evolution the original college of liberal arts faced sharply declining enrollments, yet its faculty was unwilling to compromise its intellectual integrity in the quest for higher enrollments. The faculty's response to the dilemma was the creation of a program similar to that described by Green and others, but on a much larger, college-wide scale. Parins concludes with an evaluation of the generally successful program.

The editors asked a philosopher, Ronald Jager, to provide a broad, critical analysis of the sorts of programs discussed in the three preceding essays. Jager argues that the professionalization of modern life inclines faculty as well as students to see the curriculum in utilitarian terms rather than in terms of our cultural heritage. Jager's argument is a profoundly disturbing one, for he implies that the aforementioned programs, devised to seduce students away from premature specialization and excessive concern with careers, may have the unintended consequence of reinforcing the students' vocationalism. If Jager is correct, the changes proposed in this volume are not nearly fundamental enough. Perhaps only when the crucial purpose of American higher education ceases to be certification, when grades are either eliminated or become a confidential matter between student and professor, will utilitarianism be banished from the academy.

The final chapter consists of the editors' concluding comments and a section that provides information on obtaining examples of program components described in this volume: handbooks and other sources of career information for undergraduates, career paths, career-development course syllabi, internships, and so forth.

Charles S. Green III
Richard G. Salem
Editors

References

Ackerman, J. S. "Introduction to the Issue 'The Future of the Humanities.'" *Daedalus*, 1969, *98* (3), 605–614.

Associated Press. "Economics Courses Popular with Students." *The Janesville Gazette*, December 12, 1979, p. 27.

Brown, W. R., and Allen, W. A. "Three Urgent Needs of Sociology." *The Southern Sociologist*, 1979, *10*, 18–20.

Coleman, J. S. "How Do the Young Become Adults?" *Review of Education Research*, 1972, *42* (4), 431–39.

Dayton, P. "Point of View." *The Chronicle of Higher Education*, May 29, 1979, *18*, p. 80.

Dieter, H. "Point of View: The Big Shift in Students' Majors." *The Chronicle of Higher Education*, October 20, 1980, p. 21.

Ebersole, M. C. "Why the Liberal Arts Will Survive." *The Chronicle of Higher Education*, May 21, 1979, *18*, p. 48.

Green, C. S., Klug, H., Neider, L., and Salem, R. "Coping with Vocationalism: Careerism versus Humanism in the Undergraduate Curriculum." Paper presented at annual meetings of the American Sociological Association, 1980.

Hansen, R. A., Stivers, D. J., and Francis, R. G. "Student Power and Academic Destandardization." *College Student Journal*, 1976, *10*, 217–225.

Ivins, M. "Panel Seeking Ways to Save the West's 'Awesome Space.'" *The New York Times*, June 30, 1980, p. 8.

Middleton, L. "Humanities Face Hard Struggle in 2-year Colleges." *The Chronicle of Higher Education*, November 13, 1979, *19*, p. 3.

Munschauer, J. L. "Are Liberal Arts Graduates Good for Anything?" *The Chronicle of Higher Education*, September 10, 1979, *18*, p. 48.

Riesman, D. "Ten Years On." *The New Republic*, July 1, 1978, 13–17.

Sherman, L. W. *The Quality of Police Education*. Washington, D.C.: National Advisory Commission on Higher Education for Police Officers, 1978.

Terry, G. B. "Our Professional Responsibilities Toward Job Skills and Job Shopping for Our B.S. and B.A. Graduates." *The Southern Sociologist*, 1979, *10*, 3–6.

United States National Center for Education Statistics, Office of Education, Department of Health, Education, and Welfare. *Digest of Education Statistics*. Washington, D.C.: U.S. Government Printing Office, 1980.

University of Wisconsin System, Office of Statewide Communications. *UW Memo*, 1979, *9* (9), 2.

Charles S. Green III is professor of sociology at the University of Wisconsin-Whitewater. His commitment to liberal learning was forged in reaction to his vocational education as an undergraduate in aeronautical engineering. Green's present scholarly interests include complex organizations, environmental sociology, social movements, stratification, and family.

Richard G. Salem is associate professor of sociology at the University of Wisconsin-Whitewater. Like Charles Green's, his commitment to liberal learning was forged in reaction to his undergraduate training in chemical engineering. His scholarship has focused on stratification and organizations and on the sociology of education, criminology, deviance, and conflict.

Despite the utilitarian, even anti-intellectual bias of the public vocational university, there was until recently a good opportunity to select liberal arts and pursue one's educational interests. What has happened during the last decade illustrates the unintended consequences of social good.

Higher Education and the American Political Economy

Edgar Litt

Liberal Education and the Public Vocational University

The origins of the public vocational university can be traced to the interlocking of relationships between higher education and government that has occurred since World War II. The forces responsible for this transformation include: the growth in attendance at public colleges and universities as compared to private ones; the hierarchical differentiation of higher education, complemented by the unequal allocation of talent, resources, and opportunity among the tiers of the hierarchy; the predominantly lower-middle-class base of the student population and the vocational choices that often dominate the public university. The vocational university can be described as "a knowledge apparatus explicitly designed to create and apply ideas and personnel that are functional to dominant national policies." It is "dependent on federal and corporate public research interests," and "modeled after the research and training institutes that have arisen since World War II.... By contrast, the internal core of the liberal arts curriculum is the mastery over political events as well as subject matter through cultivation of the rational and expressive faculties. Human concerns, not those of policy makers, are the core of liberal education" (Litt, 1969, p. 22).

New Directions for Teaching and Learning, 6, 1981

The wedding of government funding and academic bureaucratization threatens the survival of liberal education. "The public vocational university is highly amenable to social control because it is dependent upon public directions and support for its varied activities. Thus, it is probable that the critical intellectual will be replaced by the 'professional' knowledge worker whose public opinions are compartmentalized from his intellectual and occupational endeavors" (Litt, 1969, p. 156).

The liberal core of higher education, especially the social sciences and humanities, is probably more fragmented today than a decade ago. The analysis of the public vocational university just quoted was too conservative to the extent that the mushrooming of public higher education between 1963–1972 was measured against the ideas of the Anglo-Saxon university college. There are perhaps one hundred highly selective university colleges in America, mostly under private auspices, and ranging from Bowdoin to Reed and from Amherst to Yale. Here the liberal arts are paramount, taught to a highly select student body, and watched over by a faculty to whom teaching is the primary academic calling. And the alma mater of the American university college is the English idea of a university, rooted in the antiquity of the Oxford colleges or in their modern counterparts at Sussex and York. The university college idea was grafted onto the giant state university systems, for instance at Santa Cruz and at Old Westbury. But these exceptions prove the rule.

Such selective, small, teaching-oriented landmarks inadequately describe the realities of our dominant public higher education systems (enrolling 80 percent of all students) with the multiplicity of service, teaching, and research functions that make the American land-grant (or urban) university distinct animals set apart from their New England or Old England cousins. By 1970, a mammoth infusion of energy and resources had provided university places for 20 percent of the relevant age cohort in Great Britain. Yet here was a postsecondary pool barely one third that provided for in the United States (Litt and Parkinson, 1979). The antivocational bias of the Harvard and English university curricula in no way reflected the history of the giant, American, land-grant universities with their commitment to expanding opportunity and the most luxuriant variety of course offerings ever provided at public expense in the history of the Western world.

Neither the vocational university nor the intercourse with federal and state granting agencies are the current core of the peril to liberal learning. The structural developments of more than a decade ago have expanded. What needs to be reconsidered is why they appear so much more ominous today than when the University of Wisconsin, for instance, managed to combine vocational agricultural training with superb instruction in the social sciences. Given American commitment to providing educational opportunity, ranging from the community college to the elite, private college, it no longer serves us to employ the yardstick of a "pool of talent," certified by the English "A" levels and an invitation from the registrar of Haverford or Brown.

The original description of the public vocational university quoted above was also too radical in its assumption of a tight, causal link between the campus and the American political economy. It requires no apology for our outrage at the military-industrial-academic complex of the late 1960s to conclude that the American system lacks the central control mechanism to allocate human resources such as is found elsewhere. For instance, West Germany has a grid of educational and technical-training institutions that provide a clear flow of human resources to the upper reaches of the civil service and to the skilled-worker echelons in heavy industry. Sweden controls, by government fiat, the absolute number of students matriculating to medical school and their distribution by specialties. The English idea of a university—intimate, anti-urban, tutorial, collegiate, comprising arts and science—rests upon a meritocratic screening in which only a minority continue their education beyond the comprehensive schools. That this select minority now includes many more bright, working-class youngsters changes the social mix, not the absolute size, of those selected as the best and the brightest (Halsey and Trow, 1973).

The American reality is quite different. Despite the millions of dollars spent by the federal government on career education, our system has failed to devise an adequate technical-training mechanism—a fact that has put our productivity and economic well-being at peril. The Hartford Insurance Group may influence economic opportunity for University of Connecticut graduates, but they are in no way in control of these outcomes. The case is quite different in the West German states where the *Land* government plans the distribution of educational and economic outcomes with major private employers. Consequently, those who argue that Big Business or Big Government control economic outcomes for American college graduates are deficient in their knowledge of comparative practices among our democratic, Western European neighbors.

The essence of the multi-varied American higher education system is its pluralism, opportunity for mobility, and loose fit between the classroom and the marketplace unknown to their Swedish or British cousins. These revisions of our perspective force us to look beyond the "liberal idea for the elect" and the bogey of an omnipotent corporate boardroom calling shots at the campus level. There is a market mechanism at play, as the data suggest. For instance, between 1969-1979, the percentage of male college majors in the arts humanities and social sciences dropped from 22 to 16 percent of the total (the female decline was from 34 to 23 percent). By contrast, the percentage of males and females majoring in vocational subjects (business, education, engineering) rose from 42 to 48 percent and from 32 to 38 percent, respectively. Among women, who constitute the growth segment of American higher education, there were significant increases in the proportion of vocational majors, at the expense of liberal arts subjects, between 1971–1979 (*Chronicle of Higher Education*, 1978, pp. 4–5).

The data also support the point that market forces, not central control mechanisms, imperfectly influence college-major choices regarding job prospects. For instance, despite the rapid decline in teaching positions, women still constitute 72 percent of all education majors, and while the total of majors has fallen, its drop over the decade (about 20 percent) is far less than the absolute depletion of elementary and secondary teaching openings. Moreover, recent data show that having a job unrelated to one's college major is not a prime source of postgraduate dissatisfaction. And although about one third of 1977 college graduates report that they are "underemployed and would prefer a more challenging position" (a measure of job dissatisfaction), there is remarkably little variance by major—38 percent of the former English majors, but 33 percent of business graduates and 28 percent of engineers (Solmon, this volume). Unlike European systems, neither the choice of major nor job satisfaction is systematically built into the American higher education system.

Nevertheless, there is little ground for complacency among the liberal arts colleges across the country. By the end of the 1970s, just 18 percent of entering freshmen said they would major in the social sciences and humanities, whereas at the beginning of the decade, 32 percent indicated such a choice of major. Those aspiring to the physical and biological sciences stayed at about 10 percent of the total in both 1970 and 1980. Whereas in 1970, when liberal arts majors enjoyed prospective numerical parity with business, engineering, and other vocational students, by 1979 the job-related fields held a two-to-one advantage (Solmon, this volume). That the decline of the liberal arts can be accounted for by other factors (such as the growth of two-year community colleges) increases the concern rightly felt by liberal arts deans and departments across the country. To sum up, the alarming decline in liberal arts education cannot be blamed on insensitive bureaucrats within public higher education. Nor can it be laid at the feet of an omnipotent corporate realm suppressing interest in the humanities and social sciences in order to recruit its quota of accountants and computer technicians.

Higher Education as a Regulated Industry

The essential element in the decline of American liberal arts education is the pervasive and omnipresent regulation of higher education by agencies of government. Despite the utilitarian, even anti-intellectual bias of the public vocational university, there was until recently a good opportunity to select liberal arts courses and pursue one's educational interests.

What has happened during the last decade illustrates the unintended consequences of social good. By 1973, the Higher Education Act assured the pervasive role of federal government policy in determining the allocation of student and institutional aid. Affirmative action, in the name of removing unjust discrimination by race and sex, had changed from expanded opportunities to a system of mandated practices and record-keeping that absorbed immense amounts of university energy and funds. The industrialization of the public university brought forth an increase in collective bargaining contracts and arrangements. The now ubiquitous reliance on public funds for the conduct of research created its own bureaucratic logic, resulting in hordes of accountants and computer technicians required to account for the flow of federal and state dollars. The expanded federal role in higher education spawned new agencies—the National Endowment for the Arts and Humanities, the Fund for Postsecondary Education, and finally a Department of Education.

Nor was the regulation of higher education confined to the national level. Reorganization of state-controlled, public higher-education systems absorbed increasing amounts of time and resources. Boards of higher education, trustees, and federal agencies jostled each other in their eagerness to assure compliance with mandated social good. As the economy darkened and the flow of public funds was halted, the demand for social accountability from public higher education intensified. The era of social surplus gave way to the watchdog state, politically sensitive to demands on the public purse. The cumulative good to be achieved by adapting industrial-relations techniques to faculty economic concerns, and assuring students the sunshine of open records and truth in Princeton testing results gave way to the nightmare of a system strangling in its own red tape, oblivious to the teaching and research it supposedly performed.

Nor was the system one in which responsibility equaled authority. Federal agencies and the Congress mandated special dispensations for the handicapped and minorities, required affirmative-action hiring (even after there were no vacancies), and assured every constituency its place in the academic sun. Who could any longer deny that any Indian craftwork, supported by the National Arts Endowment, was not superior work? And how could Basic Educational Opportunity Grants paid to motivated and indifferent students alike be criticized when minorities received a disproportionate share of the aid? The march toward public accountability of decreasing support places an impossible burden on American colleges and universities. Reporting to many federal and state agencies, performing tasks without resources, and burdened with contradictory assignments, the energy of American universities has been drained from teaching and research into a paper revolution manned by an army of administrators and clerks. Federal agencies, such as the Occupational Safety and Health Agency, prescribe laboratory procedures down to the care of hamsters.

Meanwhile, state control intensifies as the public higher education sector is made more accountable. For instance, under reorganization in Massachusetts, a monolithic governing board is preparing to match campus fields of study with projections of the labor market. An institution producing too many teachers or English majors may be curtailed in favor of one manufacturing accountants and computer technicians.

The ascending political-economic control engulfing American higher education is that of government, for it is the federal and state purses that support our colleges and universities. Moreover, there has been a dramatic change in the political climate since the heyday of the public vocational university a decade ago.

This new climate is shaped by several factors. First, the decline in public spending is related to a perception that higher education has failed to provide the post-industrial spurt predicted by its advocates. The economic recession and the decline in scientific-technical expertise proceed apace despite the bloated nature of the education industry. Pressure from hard-pressed constituents makes it less fashionable to support higher education. Moreover, the overbuilding of campuses, including the public sector, leads to an intense struggle for scarce resources in which politicians find it difficult to make more friends than enemies. Finally, there is the inherent contradiction in the social welfare view of educational aid (highlighted by federal student aid to low-income groups) set against the need for more skilled talent capable of running a post-industrial society. The struggle between meritocratic and equalitarian norms in America lacks the central control and reconciliation available in European educational ministries. Therefore, universities are mandated to do more for social welfare purposes at the same time that there is a serious deficiency in the availability of resources and quality of educational standards.

The strangling regulation of American colleges and universities by a host of governmental agencies presents the most direct threat to the survival of liberal education, except in the selective university colleges. The reason is that the imperatives of governmental self-justification for bureaucratic activities inevitably leads to a pseudo-vocational ethos that provides neither career- nor general-educational outcomes. And the impetus for such bureaucratic behavior comes from the pseudo-equalitarian, pseudo-utilitarian ethos connecting higher education to the job market. Put differently, enormous amounts of scarce resources have been expended on campuses and programs that yield neither educational nor vocational outcomes.

The historical evolution of these developments can be traced to the monumental 1968 Higher Education Act and to the corresponding dependence on federal and state funding by the growing public higher education establishment. The legislation established the federal role in determining the distribution of resources, and the rationalization of public control sealed the fate of higher education in so far as control mechanisms were concerned. The close fit between equal opportunity measures (affirmative action, federal student grants) and the hierarchy of bureaucratic, external control is one of the neglected stories of the last decade. It took a downturn in the U.S. economy—an economy with a maze of institutional interests and public-administration techniques of cost-benefit analysis, planning, evaluation, and budgetary tools—to intensify the struggle for scarce resources.

Consequently, the impact of the growing governmental presence has been two-fold: first, a growing ratio of overhead costs to program funding. The administrative costs of universities have grown with the effort to comply with the new realities of American social policy, requiring affirmative action officers, budget experts, planners, and more administrative personnel. And this development means a diminution of teaching and research resources available for the essential functions of the university (Minter and Bowen, 1980). The second, and related, development is the rationalization of academic functions and personnel policies. Sources, ranging from social-equality pressures to the growth of contract-applied research, have combined to "lock-step" the university in a frozen bureaucratic pattern. For instance, the availability of "free" basic-research funding and faculty "merit" money illustrates this central point. In both cases, external pressures combine to reduce the discretionary powers of university officials. Consequently, the need to justify one's existence to increasingly critical, outside public agencies intensifies the constriction of basic research and teaching. The modern, public, vocational university becomes a vehicle for turning out products (students, made-to-order applied research) that supposedly satisfy its patrons in the state capital or in Washington. The emphasis is on "supposedly," for there is little evidence that the changes in internal priorities of universities have sustained consequences on the occupational outcomes experienced by their students. Nor is there much support for the proposition that made to order research has major economic consequences of the kind touted by grant and development officers. The key point is not the reality of enhanced job opportunities, but the politically satisfying appearance that increasingly scarce resources are being spent on socially utilitarian products.

It is just here that the uniqueness of the contemporary American higher education pattern needs to be elaborated. The American educational system has never made clear distinctions between vocational/career purposes and social welfare functions, namely those efforts to reduce prior exclusiveness or deprivation of discrete social groups. A close reading of the 1980 version of the Higher Education Act makes the point. In program after program there is a rhetorical equating of "social uplift" rhetoric with practical vocational goals. Increasingly, the reality base connecting the two has diminished because it is foolish to assume that a troubled political economy automatically benefits from the social justice in expanded Hispanic enrollment *and* the occupational skills of the same population. Broad-brush social utilitarianism, not specific career training or affirmative action, dominates dozens of federal mandates and budgetary allocations. There is no discrete national system analogous to the French polytechnics or to the German *Fachoschulen* in America. Nor can our postsecondary system, with its myriad of agencies and bureaucrats, survive by selecting potential talent as in the British system. Whereas the practical Swedes base their labor-market notions of education on exchanges between adult job-holders and students, the American practice is much more geared to individual fluctuating needs and career patterns. To reiterate an earlier point, there is a loose structural fit between the campus and the job in the United States.

The university is decreasingly a center of basic study and research and increasingly a conveyor belt of made-to-order student and research products. No less an authority than Jerome Wiesner, former president of the Massachusetts Institute of Technology, has lamented the decline in basic scientific research in the United States. It is hard to avoid the impression that the combination of economic constraints and social utilitarianism will continue over the decade. The impact will continue to fall heavily on the major public universities who upgraded their faculties and students during the lush 1960s. In a replay of the 1950s, one will look increasingly to that small number of private, selective institutions to provide the cultural life blood of scholarship and graduates.

The role of government is critical in all this, and the historical pattern leaves little room for optimism. Social histories of several national endowments and federal agencies make the point clearly. Moreover, there is a significant decline in the role of professional peer review in distributing federal aid and an upsurge in the dominance of agency management highly sensitive to political and budgetary constraints. The related decline in cultural donations by private foundations also contributes to the projected relative decline, which points to a more parochial, utilitarian, academic culture. Such liberal culture as remains will become increasingly expensive and available only to patrons with adequate private capital. In institutional terms, the public universities, and all but the highly endowed, private institutions, will be priced out of the dominant liberal arts market.

The Outlook: 1984 and Beyond

The enormous increase in governmental regulation of higher education is unlikely to decrease, nor are the social and political pressures from assertive interest groups demanding that governmental purse and power be brought to bear on the campus. The positive aspects of governmental intervention ought to be noted. Since 1968 we have witnessed the most massive, government-supported upgrading of social opportunity in the history of Western education. Black enrollment in colleges and universities doubled and is at parity with white enrollment among middle-class families. Women now constitute an absolute majority among college enrollees in 1980. There is hardly a governmental program touching on higher education that does not contain funds and regulations designed to continue the opportunities of minorities. Similarly, the massive opportunities available for study in liberal arts remain battered, if unbowed, in the great public higher education systems. For example, the University of Connecticut has some forty tenured English professors at salaries of approximately $35,000 each. The life-time commitment to liberal arts is perhaps $500 million when fringe benefits are computed. The liberal arts, both undergraduate and graduate, will not disappear from the American scene. However, it is a different question whether another generation of scholars, facing continued inflation and poor job prospects, will lose ground.

The more worrisome aspect is the continuation of seed funding and support for the cultivation of the mind. The percentage of American higher education faculty who have studied or taught abroad is a dismal 15 percent. In either absolute or per capita terms, the number of faculty and student Fulbrights (indeed, the amount of all aid for international study) is pathetic. For example, West Germany offers four Fulbrights to every one funded by the United States. Buried in the hundreds of socially utilitarian grants and fellowships documented in the 1980 Higher Education Act is a provision for a mere 100 graduate fellowships, unrestricted in purpose and field. The total support (faculty and student) available for social science and humanities study is less than the absolute number provided by the West Germans. There is but one source of governmental international-travel funding in Washington (at the National Science Foundation), and it provides but a fraction of the group and individual requests made upon it.

The cumulative, probable impact on liberal higher education as a regulated, depressed industry goes well beyond the paucity of international support for the next generation of teachers and scholars. The first aspect is the continued ascendency of the vocational ethos and the concomitant eclipse of the liberal arts rationale. Educational ideologies wither away when the social environment no longer provides support for their key values. It will be increasingly difficult to sustain the liberal arts ethos— even in diluted form—when job and economic pressures persistently fall upon the universities and their students.

An "iron triangle" of negative influences presses upon the liberal arts. One leg of this triangle is the long-term economic outlook facing American colleges and universities. The golden decade of the 1960s will not reappear. Faced with enrollment and resource difficulties, universities will continue to adapt to their constricted and less friendly environment.

The second leg of the triangle is the continued effort to market vocational and job-related skills and programs. This effort is already changing the core humanities and social science curriculum at the undergraduate and graduate levels. The move is toward an applied, business-like direction in which marketable skills become the first order of course offerings and degree programs. There are two key issues here: First, the success of the liberal arts in the fierce struggle for scarce resources, in which their move toward vocational status confronts the genuine, established articles in the schools of business, engineering, pharmacy, and so forth. Second, even some measure of success in a mutation to practicality runs directly into the second order problem—will the adaptation of the liberal arts to the world of job relevance cause the loss of those sensibilities that have sustained the humanities throughout Western civilization and the social sciences since the nineteenth century? Will emphasis on business English eventually eradicate the study of literature? Will preoccupation with applied public service and administration lead to the disappearance of the core ideas that have advanced the study of society—from Freud to Erik Erikson and from Marx to Daniel Bell?

Finally, the triangle engulfing the liberal arts is completed by the unrelenting regulation of the government—at federal, state, and local levels. Political change and bureaucracies are seldom undone. The massive increase in governmental oversight of all aspects of university life will continue because it is now fully institutionalized in the essential processes of our universities and colleges.

There are subsidiary problems that could also be considered—the aging, almost fully tenured faculties without room for new, young blood at the lower ranks; the dependence on the whims and variations of extramural (mainly governmental) funding sources.

But despite the adversities, the spirit of liberal education endures. It endures in the quest to explore the unknown and in the highly professional and resilient character of the faculty. It endures in the conviction that only through liberal learning can students acquire those conceptual, analytical, and communicative abilities that are crucial for coping with the personal challenges posed by the changing job market and with the challenges our world faces in the future.

It is for these reasons that the negative influences may not obliterate the legacy of arts and literature and the foundations of social knowledge which provide us the choice of either shaping our environment constructively or permitting it to destroy us in conflict.

References

Bell, D. *The Coming of the Post-industrial Society.* New York: Basic Books, 1972.
Carnegie Foundation for the Advancement of Teaching. *More than Survival: Prospects for Higher Education in a Period of Uncertainty.* San Francisco: Jossey-Bass, 1975.

Chronicle of Higher Education, January 1978, pp. 4–5.

Driver, C. *The Exploding University*. London: Hodder and Stockton, 1971.

Halsey, A. H., and Trow, M. A. *The British Academics*. London: Faber and Faber, 1973.

Litt, E. *The Public Vocational University: Captive Knowledge and Public Power*. New York: Holt, Rinehart and Winston, 1969.

Litt, E. "Successes and Failures of Equal Opportunity Programs in the U.S." In *British Society for Research into Higher Education: Proceedings*. London: British Society for Research into Higher Education, 1974.

Litt, E. "Figging the Levellers." *The Chronicle of Higher Education*, March 24, 1976, p. 33.

Litt, E., and Parkinson, M. *U.S. and U.K. Education Policy: A Decade of Reform*. New York: Praeger, 1979.

Melanson, P. *Knowledge, Politics, and Public Policy*. Cambridge, Mass.: Winthrop Press, 1976.

Minter, E. J., and Bowen, H. A. *Preserving America's Investment in Human Capital*. Washington, D.C.: American Association of State Colleges and Universities, 1980.

Spring, J. *National Education Policy Since 1945*. New York: McKay, 1976.

Thomas, N. *Education in National Politics*. New York: McKay, 1975.

Edgar Litt is professor of political science
at the University of Connecticut. He is the author
of numerous works on the political sociology
of higher education, including, most recently,
U.S. and U.K. Education Policy: A Decade of Reform
(with M. Parkinson).

*Longitudinal studies of two cohorts of
entering freshmen refute the belief by some that
there is presently "too much" higher education
in this country.*

Exploring the Link Between College Education and Work

Lewis C. Solmon

Until 1970, the ability of the educational system to prepare students for jobs
was so widely accepted that support for education was based largely on
manpower needs. To the general public, more schooling meant better jobs.
The educators assured the nation that manpower needs would be met in
time of national crisis (for example, scientists for defense and space programs) and personal need (for example, service workers for industry, the
home, and health-care fields).

During the 1970s, however, students, faculty, and educational
policy-makers have questioned the usefulness of postsecondary education
in work. Postsecondary education has become almost commonplace, with
over 60 percent of high school graduates enrolling in traditional two- and
four-year colleges and many more continuing their studies in vocational
programs. Manpower shortages are evident in certain occupations, while
surpluses appear in others. Some people claim that higher education no
longer ensures a good job or, in some cases, any job at all, and that too many
college graduates are forced to take jobs that do not use their education.

By now, almost no one is shocked to hear about the exponential
growth in American higher education enrollments over the last twenty-five
years. In 1955, 2.6 million people were enrolled in colleges and universities.
By 1975, this figure had increased to 11.2 million (U.S. Department of

Health, Education, and Welfare, 1978). In 1950, 6.2 million people (age twenty-five or older) had a bachelor's degree or higher. By 1975, 13.9 million people had at least a bachelor's degree (U.S. Bureau of the Census, 1976). In twenty-five years, then, the number of college graduates in the work force more than doubled. Unfortunately, however, the rate of increase in the number of jobs traditionally filled by people with a college education did not keep pace with the rate of college-degree production—the supply of graduates exceeded their demand in the labor market. Forecasts to the mid 1980s do not indicate any relief. The Bureau of Labor Statistics (1973), for example, projects that only about one fifth of all jobs in 1980 will "require" a college education, leaving as many as two and one-half college graduates competing for every "choice" job: Choice jobs, apparently, are those that require a college education.

Underemployment

Based on these and similar figures, educators, researchers, policy-makers, and students have been bemoaning the problems of underemployment and overeducation. For most economists, who view education as a human capital investment, the problem of too many college graduates for too few commensurate jobs is one of overeducation (Freeman, 1976). The imbalanced market will adjust itself in time; surpluses will become shortages and then surpluses again in a cyclical fashion as the word about job opportunities filters down to freshmen (Freeman, 1971). Students react to the job market, but their adjustments are not felt for about four years, the time between college entry and graduation.

For other social scientists, the problem is one of underemployment, not overeducation (O'Toole, 1977). They argue that students should not have to adjust to the market by changing their major field or by not enrolling in college at all. Instead, employers should redesign jobs to accommodate the more highly educated labor pool. As in most controversies, neither view is completely wrong or right. Some workers will slowly adjust to the market, and some employers will see the advantages of making previously unchallenging jobs more challenging.

The debate on the value of college education for work remains unresolved. Richard Freeman (1976) observed a decline in the relative income advantage of college graduates compared with high school graduates, and from this inferred that Americans are overeducated. David Witmer, however, disputes these findings (Witmer, 1978a; 1978b). Ivar Berg (1971) declared that 80 percent of college graduates have jobs previously filled by workers with lower education credentials. Consequently, college training does not have the same employment benefits it had in the past. Finally, O'Toole (1975; 1977) predicted that a new meritocracy will develop, wherein the 20 percent with all the good jobs will be confronted by the 80 percent with the bad jobs. He fears that the 80 percent will challenge the right of the 20 percent to have special privileges and that the "reserve army of the underemployed" may rise against the new meritocracy.

But before anyone—students, educators, workers, employers—does anything about the situation, it must be determined what can or should be done. The job market is not static; that is what makes manpower forecasting such a hazardous business (Gordon, 1974). That is also why many educators advocate the liberal arts rather than vocational training. A liberal arts graduate, they say, can be flexible enough to adapt to a changing world. Non-liberal arts graduates face the increasingly serious possibility of skill obsolescence. Workers with specific skills may be more successful than their more generally prepared counterparts in finding related jobs at first, but, later in their lives, they may find themselves enrolling in job-retraining programs as many as six or seven times.

The problem is that most campus recruiters are looking for business, accounting, and engineering majors rather than liberal arts majors. Corporate presidents, many of whom were trained in the humanities, advocate hiring the latter, but few presidents actually do any hiring. In past generations, the mere possession of a college degree was a prestigious enough credential to propel those who earned it into top positions. Today, screening is more likely to be by grades, institutional quality, and field of study. Indeed, it may be more logical to edit the writings of a scientist-manager than to train a humanist-manager on-the-job in the technical knowledge required for successful administration.

The question is: How well do the colleges and universities perform their vocational role, assuming that preparation for work is an important legitimate role for them? For the past ten years the critics have charged higher education with a poor performance. It is argued that too many college graduates, particularly from the humanities, are underemployed and that the outlook is dim.

The Data Bases Used in this Study

Scope of the 1974 Study. These opinions about the relationship between education and work were questioned in a recent study conducted by the Higher Education Research Institute (HERI) (Bisconti and Solmon, 1976, 1977; and Solmon, Bisconti, and Ochsner, 1977). This study involved a 1974 follow-up of freshmen enrolled in 1961 who had responded to the Cooperative Institutional Research Program's (CIRP) freshman survey. This group of freshmen was also surveyed in 1965 and 1971.* The 1961

---

*The Cooperative Institutional Research Program, sponsored by the American Council on Education and the University of California, Los Angeles, is directed by Alexander W. Astin, professor of higher education at UCLA and presi-

CIRP freshmen had been working full time for up to ten years by the time of the 1974 follow-up.

The 1974–1961 study focused on undergraduate education. Consequently, only bachelor's degree holders were surveyed. The analyses were further limited to those working full time and to whites (because of an insufficient number in other racial-ethnic groups for separate analyses). The analyses, then, were based on the responses of a total 4,840 people. (In subsequent discussions, this group of respondents will be referred to as the 1974 cohort.)

Two major questions guided the investigation: How closely related are the jobs to the major field of these college graduates? and, How satisfied are they with their jobs? Almost half the sample responded that they hold closely related jobs and only 25 percent said they held completely unrelated jobs. More than half the sample (57 percent) were very satisfied with their jobs, whereas only 4 percent were not at all satisfied. Of the 26 percent who held unrelated jobs, fewer than 5 percent held them involuntarily. Furthermore, only 26 percent of those college graduates who held unrelated jobs involuntarily were completely dissatisfied. One major conclusion of the study, therefore, was that having a job unrelated to one's college major is not in itself sufficient cause for dissatisfaction. This may not seem so important until it is realized that the definition of underemployment, as used in much of the recent literature about the scarcity of jobs for college graduates, involves the lack of match between job and major, or at least between years of education obtained and years of education required for the particular job.

The study concluded that, after seven to nine years in the labor force, a large number of college graduates were still using, on the job, knowledge they had gained in college and that the majority were very satisfied with their jobs. Most respondents in unrelated jobs held their jobs voluntarily, and the relationship of job to major had little to do with job satisfaction. These results contradict conclusions by researchers such as O'Toole, Freeman, and Berg, who observed that few jobs are available that enable college students to use their training, that underemployment of college graduates is widespread, and that this leads to worker dissatisfaction.

Several characteristics of the 1974–1961 cohort led to questions about the relevance of the results to more recent graduates. In particular, those who had participated in the study had been working for approxi-

dent of the Higher Education Research Institute. The 1961 survey was conducted at the National Merit Scholarship Corporation, Evanston, Illinois. For a full account of the freshman four-year follow-up surveys, see Astin and Panos (1969). The 1971 survey methodology and findings are reported in El-Khawas and Bisconti (1974), and Bisconti and Astin (1973). The 1974 survey methodology and findings are reported in Solmon, Bisconti, and Ochsner (1977), and Bisconti and Solmon (1976, 1977).

mately nine years, and had entered the labor force about 1965. The year 1965 was characterized by a much lower unemployment rate than more recent years. The overall unemployment rate was 4.5 percent in 1965 and 8.3 percent in 1976 (U.S. Bureau of the Census, 1976). For college graduates in the age twenty to twenty-four category, the unemployment rate was 4.7 percent in 1965, dropping to under 2 percent in 1967, but then increasing in the 1970s to over 8 percent in 1977 (U.S. Bureau of Labor Statistics, 1966, 1968, 1978). Clearly, the 1961 freshmen entered the labor force when the economy was much stronger than it is today.

Another difference between the employment situation in 1965 and more recent times is indicated by those entering the labor force with new bachelor's degrees. Some 501,000 of these degrees were awarded in 1965, but the number grew to 925,000 by 1976.

Assuming that a stronger economy can better use baccalaureate talent, the number of bachelor's recipients per dollar of Gross National Product (GNP) per capita (adjusted for price-level changes) is a good measure of the economy's absorption capacity. This ratio results in figures of 97.1 in 1960, 112.9 in 1965, 168.2 in 1970, and 176.3 in 1975. By converting these figures into indices to measure the ability of the economy to absorb new bachelor's degree recipients, and by giving the 1960 figures a value of one, we can determine that the 1976 index is 1.816. That is, over 80 percent more bachelor's degree holders per dollar of GNP per capita were available for jobs in 1976 than in 1960. The 1965 index is much closer to the one for 1960 than for 1976.

The 1974–1961 survey was replicated in 1977 by the Higher Education Research Institute, when a sample of 1970 college freshmen was surveyed. They had entered the labor force around 1974–1975, during much less favorable times. (This group of respondents will be referred to in subsequent discussions as the 1977 cohort.) Overall, the results of the more recent study corroborate the most significant conclusions from the earlier study, although there are slight differences.

The 1977 Study. Questionnaires were sent to 28,549 of the 180,000 CIRP respondents of 1970.* An attempt was made to oversample those 1970 respondents who aspired to a bachelor's degree or less, were black, were freshmen at two-year colleges, and anticipated majoring in the humanities. Of the 28,549 surveyed, 3,842 men and 5,197 women responded, an overall response rate of 31.7 percent. Adjusting for the number of nondeliverable questionnaires (6,194), however, resulted in a 40.4 percent response rate—a very hearty one for this type of survey.**

*The 1977–1970 survey was funded by the National Institute of Education (Grant No. 76–0080). Supplemental funds were also provided by the Rockefeller Foundation and the College Placement Council (CPC) Foundation.

**A more detailed discussion of the survey procedures is available from the Higher Education Research Institute, 924 Westwood Boulevard, Suite 835, Los Angeles, CA 90024.

Since the 1974 follow-up study of the 1961 freshmen (Solmon, Bisconti, and Ochsner, 1977) was based on a sample of white respondents who had received the bachelor's but no advanced degree and were employed full time, this study of 1970 freshmen was designed to be an analysis of the sample that fits those three criteria (white, bachelor's degree holders, full-time employed). (However, the respondents did include enough people with less than a bachelor's degree to enable comparisons by years of schooling obtained for this paper.) A separate analysis of the small number of blacks in the sample would be almost meaningless without weighting their responses. The response rate for blacks was much lower than for whites—only 13 percent. Even though blacks were oversampled, they underresponded. The present analyses, then, are based on the responses of 5,428 people. For both cohorts, however, numbers may vary slightly due to lack of responses to specific questions.

Although the two studies were designed to parallel each other as closely as possible, there are several notable differences that could affect comparisons between the 1974–1961 and 1977–1970 cohorts. The first one, already noted, is that differences in opportunity to use college training and in job satisfaction might be a function of the different labor market conditions at the time graduates first entered the labor force. Even if one minimized the effect of labor market conditions when the two cohorts began working, the economy was much stronger in 1974, the time of follow-up of the 1961 freshmen, than in 1977, the time of follow-up of the 1970 freshmen. For example, the unemployment rate in March 1974 for all college graduates was 1.9 percent, whereas, in March 1977, it was 3.3 percent or almost 50 percent higher (U.S. Bureau of Labor Statistics, 1975, 1978).

Another difference is that the 1977 follow-up obtained information on job attitudes of individuals who had been working for three years or less, whereas the 1974 follow-up obtained perspectives from those who had been in the labor force for approximately nine years. It is generally agreed that it takes five to ten years for an individual to achieve long-run career aspirations. For example, in the first years of work, individuals tend to obtain on-the-job training (Mincer, 1970) and to experiment with various career options. These activities usually result in lower levels of job satisfaction (U.S. Department of Labor, 1974) and in more negative attitudes about the value of education than those revealed later in life. Hence, the length of time in the labor force may account, in part, for differences between the 1974 and 1977 responses.

Measures of Overeducation

Although many arguments have been put forth to support the "overeducated American" view (Freeman, 1976), there have been at least as many attempts at rebuttal (Rumberger, 1980; Smith and Welch, 1978). This chapter will bypass most of this discussion in order to provide new data on two of the most important measures of overeducation. The first question is whether the payoff in income for a college education is still as great as it has been in the past, or even if it still pays at all to go to college. Since our sample is dominated by people who have attended college, there is some difficulty in answering this question. However, the richness of the data base will enable us to develop some new insights. The second question concerns the match between educational attainments and job requirements of the college-educated work force, and here our data do seem to enlighten previous discussions significantly.

Income

The standard human-capital model enables us to compare rates of return to years of schooling by regressing the log of income on years of education along with other appropriate determinants of or correlates with human-capital production, such as work experience, sex, marital status, religion, aspects of education (like major, grades and college quality) and job characteristics. The HERI data bases have the limitation that for 1974 we can compare only earnings of those with bachelor's degrees to those with higher degrees, and for 1977 the comparisons are only among those with some college but less than a bachelor's, a bachelor's, and more than a bachelor's degree. Nevertheless, we have a variety of other college-related measures that can be tested for their relationship to annual income. Additionally, we are able to control for effects of employment sector, length of employment since leaving school (work experience), whether or not the respondent was self-employed, sex, marital status, and religion. (Since the mathematical formulation of the relevant earnings function has been reproduced in hundreds of articles in the past decade, we will not do it here.)

Estimation of the earnings model for the 1977 cohort reveals strong effects of years of schooling. The size of the coefficients are comparable to those obtained recently by Rumberger (1980), who used 1975 CPS data. (The coefficients obtained here are somewhat smaller since those with bachelor's degrees or 17+ years of schooling are compared to those with some college rather than to people with a high school degree.) It appears that, in 1977, for those who entered college in 1970, there was a substantial earnings advantage if they completed college and or had post-undergraduate education as well. It also appears that there was an additional payoff according to the quality of the institution attended (measured by selectivity; Astin and Henson, 1977): Those who attended private colleges were earning less than those who had attended public institutions, but this is out of the effect of selectivity and grades. There was a clear payoff for grades, with A students earning 3.6 percent more and C students 6.3 percent less than what B students earned.

Finally, major field was revealed to have significant impact on earnings. Arts, humanities, and social science graduates were at the bottom of the income ladder, with engineering and professional majors at the top, and business majors next.

Thus, it appears that for those who entered college at the start of the 1970s, income in the early years of employment (average work experience for the 1977 cohort was thirty-two months) was related positively to years of education, quality of college attended, grades, and major. This is consistent with both the human-capital theory and with new versions of sorting models. The latter argue that in earlier times merely obtaining high levels (years) of education produced sufficient human capital to justify superior wages. Recently, when as many as 70 percent of the cohort of high school graduates entered some college or other, employers could no longer be certain that college attendance alone indicated high potential for productivity. This is due in part to the fact that the curriculum at many colleges has been diluted to provide remediation to students able to attend only because of open admissions. Thus employers place more emphasis on where one went to college, progress therein, grades, and field (engineers, for example, are assumed to be brighter than English majors).

Although the earnings regression for the 1977 cohort alone cannot directly refute the "overeducated American" arguments, it does clearly indicate that the nature of post-secondary education does make a difference in earnings. And these results hold after controlling for employment sector, sex, length of employment, marital status, and religion.

An earning function for 1961 college freshmen based on 1974 data was also estimated. However, since the minimum educational attainment for this sample was a bachelor's degree, the only effect of years of schooling that can be discerned is between those with bachelor's degrees and those with additional years of education. It is clear that for those with about seven years of work experience (average experience of the 1974 cohort was eighty-four months), there was a payoff for education beyond the bachelor's degree. Moreover, the effect of quality of college attended (again selectivity) was large, indeed larger than for the younger cohort. Although the size of this coefficient might be biased upward due to the unavailability of information on grades in college (and grades are correlated positively with selectivity of college attended), the fact that college quality has a greater impact on earnings after a longer time in the labor force is consistent with earlier studies by the author (Solmon, 1973).

It is noteworthy that major field still seems to affect earnings after seven years of work. Business and social science degrees seem to increase in value over time, while the initial payoff of engineering degrees diminishes somewhat.

In summary, it is obvious that the earnings regressions for 1977 and 1974 are not a clear and direct test of the declining relative-income argument for the "overeducated American" theory. Our two cohorts have different years of work experience, different control variables are available for the two regressions, and, most troublesome, neither group includes members who did not attend college. (For the 1974 cohort, the following control variables were unavailable: professional major, grades, education less than a bachelor's degree, and religious preference.) It is clear, however, that for the two groups of college attenders, college experiences and achievements are significant factors in income determination. Surely postsecondary education mattered (in terms of income) during the time Richard Freeman's data were being produced (1971, 1976).

The Links Between Job Requirements and Educational Skills

Many social scientists, and particularly economists, eschew asking direct questions on surveys; they prefer indirect measures. For example, data on job satisfaction are often inferred from "objective" data on turnover rates rather than collected from data by asking workers how satisfied they are. The fact that many successful and satisfied workers change jobs because they are offered better ones is ignored. The direct approach, it is argued, is wrought with problems of measurement error: cognitive dissonance, whereby workers may not answer honestly (for example, compared to being a garbage man, one's dissatisfying job may be okay).

More to the point of the "overeducated American" debate is the way it has been shown that college graduates are taking jobs that demand fewer skills than they possess. In general, the approach has been to determine the educational requirements of jobs from some "objective" determination by the U.S. Department of Labor (Berg, 1971; O'Toole, 1975, 1977). What is left unsaid is how the Department of Labor collects these "objective data." Job requirements are determined by asking employers what the *minimum* educational requirements are for a job. If the employer says, for example, that he would never hire a secretary with less than an eleventh grade education, any secretary with more education than that is said to be overeducated, or underemployed. Even if *minimum* requirements were changed to *average* requirements, there is a direct assumption that those in jobs with above average education are overeducated.

A more recent example of this approach is that of Rumberger (1980). "Overeducation attempts to account directly for the utilization of educational skills in the labor market" (p. 110). And "The Employment Service periodically collects information on the characteristics of jobs in the U.S. economy, including information on general skill requirements [*Dictionary of Occupations Titles*]. These requirements are supposedly determined solely from the tasks of the job and not the characteristics of the worker in the jobs. *But it is by no means a perfect system* (emphasis added). For the purposes of this paper, though, we will assume the independence between educational attainments and skill requirements. Another limitation of this approach is its failure to account for changes in skill requirements over time. It is reasonable to assume that skill requirements of a job rise or fall as the tasks of the job change; however, such a change is unlikely to be substantial over such a short period. The results understate (overstate) the amount of overeducation to the degree that the skill requirements of jobs have decreased (increased) during the period" (p. 104).

To restate the problem: It is assumed that there are distinct jobs wherein educational requirements are homogeneous. Jobs do not change as the educational attainment of the incumbent changes. Years of education measure relevant skills possessed by individuals; that is, one with more years of schooling has more job-related skills than one with less, even if the college graduate majored in engineering and the Ph.D. studied Latin. Finally, job requirements are learned either from employers or from "objective analyses of job tasks," *but rarely if ever by asking those who are working in the jobs.*

Our data represent a radical departure from this approach. We wanted to learn if college education was useful in work, so we asked workers. Certainly the workers could have lied when they answered. But with large samples and with multiple questions on the same topic, we believe our results are more reliable than results from the indirect approach.

Measures of Work-Education Links

For the younger (1977) cohort, 56 percent said their jobs were closely related to their major, 19 percent said their jobs were somewhat related, and 25 percent said their jobs were not at all related. As would be expected, the match between job and major was lower for those who had been in the work force longer (for the 1974 cohort, 46 percent said closely related, 27 percent said somewhat, and 26 percent said not at all). By the time college graduates have been working for seven to nine years, many have moved into management positions or into other functions with more general responsibilities than those prepared for in college. The most conclusive test of the changing utilization would have been a comparison of a younger and older group of graduates when they had been working for the same number of years. Unfortunately, the data for these comparisons are not available. But the fact remains that in the second half of the 1970s, only one in four recent college graduates saw little or no relationship between their major and their job.

More importantly, perhaps, are the reasons given by those not in closely related jobs for holding such positions. It is clear that the younger group is more likely to be in non-related jobs for involuntary reasons: "employment opportunities are scarce for people in jobs related to my major" (50 percent vs. 22 percent), and "could not get a closely related job but would prefer one" (36 percent vs. 8 percent). Similarly, the older cohort was more likely to be holding unrelated jobs for voluntary reasons: "prefer line of work not closely related" (24 percent vs. 11 percent of the younger group), and "tried closely related employment, but did not like" (20 percent vs. 8 percent). Thus there seems to be some evidence that the link between work and education is weakening, even though only one quarter of each group is in unrelated jobs.

Regression analysis was used to isolate factors associated with the perception of the relationships between job and major for each cohort separately. (The dependent variable has three values: three equals closely related, two equals somewhat related, and one equals not at all related.) More years of schooling lead to a closer link for the 1977 cohort, but for the 1974 cohort, there is no significant difference between those with bachelor's degrees and those with seventeen or more years of schooling. For the younger group, those with higher grades appear to have more opportunity to use their training; and women are less likely to be in related jobs. For the older cohort only, the people who attended more selective and private colleges are more likely to have moved (been promoted perhaps) into unrelated jobs. It is also clear that field and employment sector are strongly related to the relation of job to major for both cohorts. Those who majored in business, engineering, or professional fields are more likely to be in related jobs, but this link is weaker after seven to nine years of work. Most other majors are less likely to be in related jobs and the likelihood is even smaller (that is, the negative coefficients are larger) for arts, humanities, and social science majors after seven years. And it is in teaching where education-job links are strongest. It is also interesting that in the corporate, government, and military employment sectors, those who have worked longer are more likely to see a link with their majors. It seems that some college graduates begin to perceive the value of college only after working for some time. At the beginning, the relationship question seems to be evaluated according to the degree of *direct* application of course materials, whereas after obtaining work experience, the relationship is viewed in terms of the ability to apply the *broad* set of skills and competencies acquired during the college years.

This point is demonstrated by the fact that use of major and minor courses is greater for the younger group (54 percent of the younger cohort used their major courses "almost always/frequently," compared to 45 percent of the older cohort), although use of "other" courses does not change over time (21 percent of both cohorts said they used their other undergraduate courses "almost always/frequently"). The same pattern emerged when the use of college courses in work was examined by sex. However, when considering differences by major, it appears that those in English, economics, and business are more likely to see a stronger link after more years of work. All other majors—arts and humanities, social sciences, engineering—were perceived to be more useful to younger workers. Those who possess communication, writing, and business skills seem to have more opportunity to use these once they have made progress in their careers. Thus it seems unreasonable to evaluate overeducation or under-employment, first, without differentiating by major, and second, by looking only at entry-level jobs rather than jobs held after some period of time. These deficiencies are obvious in the work of Freeman and his supporters.

There are other ways a college education can be useful in employment. The older workers are slightly more likely to recognize that college increased their general knowledge (73 percent of the 1974 cohort vs. 70 percent of the 1977 cohort). They were also more likely to feel college increased their chances of finding a good job (69 percent of the older group vs. 61 percent of the younger group), a reasonable premise given the proliferation of college degrees in recent years. However, the younger group valued more highly all the other contributions—"gave knowledge and skills used in current job, helped choose life goals, increased leadership ability," and so forth. A naive interpretation of these data would be that recent college graduates have benefited more from college than has the older group. This would clearly contradict arguments about the declining value of college. More realistically, it is likely that by the time college attenders have been working for seven to nine years, they recognize that other (non-college) factors have become more important in their career progress, and that college experiences alone are insufficient.

Regression analysis was used to explain individual differences in responses to the question of the extent to which college gave knowledge and skills used in the current job. For both cohorts, the more years in school, the more likely postsecondary education was to have this positive effect. However, the impact was greater for the younger group. Selectivity was not significant for the younger group but had a negative impact for the 1974 cohort. In both years, attending a private institution was negatively related to this impact as well. This confirms the stronger vocational orientation of less selective and public colleges. Finally, the dummy variables distinguishing among majors and employment sectors had the expected effects.

Another important paradox in the discussion of overeducation deserves unravelling. Two questions were asked of members of the HERI survey panel: one about the relationship of job to major, and one about their perception of whether or not one's skills were fully used on the job. For both cohorts, being in a closely related job does not necessarily imply full skill utilization. That is, the latter is evaluated by considering a whole set of skills and competencies (that is, human capital), some acquired by formal schooling, some innate, and some acquired outside the school or college setting (for example, on-the-job training, leisure activities). Over 55 percent of those from each cohort who hold jobs related to their majors do not feel that their skills are fully used. This finding leads to the observation that problems of underemployment are probably independent of any failure of the colleges to provide training relevant to work. Even when the college-work links exist, there are likely to be underused skills. Hence any inference that colleges are not doing their job seems somewhat beside the point.

Unfortunately, the direct question of whether or not respondents feel underemployed was asked only in 1977. However, given the arguments that recent college graduates are underemployed, the data are highly relevant. Underemployment seems to vary significantly according to college major. Education, engineering, and economics majors are least likely to feel underemployed (40 percent and less), whereas humanities and other social science majors are most likely to feel this way (over half). And the range of those who are underemployed and would prefer a more challenging position is from 17 percent of education majors to 38 to 39 percent of humanities and social science majors.

Here we have a question analogous to whether the glass is half empty or half full. Given that (1) underemployment clearly refers to use of skills and talent *in addition* to those acquired in college; (2) many, particularly humanities and social science majors, attend college for many reasons in addition to the desire for a good job; (3) the benefits of college are much broader than merely job-related ones (see, for example, Bowen, 1977); and (4) given all this, under 40 percent indicate that they are underemployed and would prefer a more challenging position, can we say that colleges are becoming less valuable institutions? Obviously, we would prefer that no college graduate feel underemployed. But if this were accomplished at the cost of artificially "creating" college-level jobs (whatever that means), would the social costs exceed the benefits?

Job Satisfaction

Perhaps the best summary statistic on the job-related effectiveness of college education is the satisfaction of college graduates with their jobs. A higher percentage of the more experienced workers are very satisfied (57 percent of the 1974 cohort vs. 44 percent of the 1977 cohort) and a smaller share of that group are not at all satisfied (4 percent of the 1974 cohort vs. 14 percent of the 1977 cohort). At first, this seems to support those who argue that the quality of jobs obtained by college graduates is declining. But it is inappropriate to compare satisfaction of older and younger workers at one time and to conclude that dissatisfaction is growing because the younger workers are less satisfied. A survey of many research studies by the U.S. Department of Labor (1974) indicates that younger workers are *always* more dissatisfied with their jobs than older, more experienced workers are. And this is true despite the greater use of their education by the younger workers. It might be argued that cognitive dissonance sets in after a while. However, we prefer the explanation that new entrants into the labor force are unsettled in their careers, disappointed when they are not given important responsibilities right from the start, required to spend most of their time learning on-the-job, and intimidated when they realize how little they really do know. After five or ten years, workers achieve a position on a true career path and become productive, and so their satisfaction increases. If this analysis is correct, it must again be concluded that those who evaluate the usefulness of college for work by looking at new entrants are simply missing the point.

Even so, only 4 percent of the 1974 cohort expressed dissatisfaction, but 14 percent of the 1977 cohort said they were not satisfied. Fourteen percent is far from the 80 percent speculated by O'Toole and others to be underemployed and therefore greatly dissatisfied. It must be noted, however, that this study considered only full-time workers, whereas O'Toole and others probably considered part-timers as well.

Our data enable us to discern several of the underlying relationships between job satisfaction and the variables discussed earlier:

1. Although those holding jobs closely related to their major are more likely than others to feel this is important, large numbers of workers, regardless of the relationship between their job and major, do not feel the relationship is important.

2. Those who are holding unrelated jobs for voluntary reasons are as satisfied as those in closely related jobs. Only those involuntarily engaged in unrelated jobs are less satisfied, and even among this small group, fewer than half are not at all satisfied.

3. For men and women in each cohort, for a given degree of relatedness, there is a positive relationship between salary and job satisfaction. However, for a given level of job satisfaction, salary levels do not vary by degree of relatedness of job to major.

4. On a number of attitudes (such as "would like to remain with current employer for foreseeable future, job fits long-range goals," and so forth) and job characteristics (such as "have sufficient status or prestige in job, design own work program," and so forth), the older group appears more satisfied than the younger group. However, most of the differences can be explained by position in the career cycle rather than by anything else, including the role of college in job preparation.

5. For the 1977 cohort, the most satisfying jobs are those that offer challenge, status, income, and opportunities for advancement.

6. The only college-related characteristic that predicts job satisfaction is selectivity for the 1977 cohort. Length of employment has a positive coefficient for both samples. Humanities majors and young workers in the corporate sector are less satisfied than others.

7. Relationship of job to major does not predict job satisfaction, but whether or not skills are fully used is very important. This implies that skills not acquired in college should be tapped by employers as much as possible.

Conclusion

This chapter has drawn upon the results of two follow-up surveys of college freshmen to obtain some insights relevant to the "overeducated American" debate. Ideally, it would have been best to have data both on people with high school as their highest educational attainment and people who attended college, but only data on college attenders was available. Since the two groups entered the labor force in different economic eras, one group had about five years more experience at the time of the follow-up survey. Nevertheless, the results appear informative.

Years of college attendance, attributes of college attended, and student achievements therein still affected earnings in the late 1970s. Very few recent college graduates are involuntarily holding jobs unrelated to their college training. This is very much dependent upon the major field. Recent graduates value college in a variety of job-related ways. Most workers are more concerned with using all their talents than they are about use of what they learned in school. Underemployment and job dissatisfaction are less pervasive than many researchers would have us believe. And it seems clear that the efficacy of college cannot be evaluated by looking solely at labor market outcomes during the first few years in the labor force.

Finally, our results seem to be corroborated by decisions of students regarding choice of major over the decade of the 1970s. (Every fall, the Cooperative Institutional Research Program asks freshmen about their possible major field. Their preferences are a predictor of subsequent enrollment in specific fields. Among the data from a national norms series [1966 to 1979] sponsored jointly by the American Council on Education and the Graduate School of Education, UCLA, and under the direction of Alexander W. Astin, are the percentages of first-time, full-time freshmen who selected various majors.) There have been precipitous declines in the share of arts and humanities and mathematics majors throughout the period, (from 13 percent in 1970 to 8 percent in 1979 for arts and humanities majors, and from 3 percent in 1970 to 1 percent in 1979 for math majors), whereas majors in education, social sciences, and physical and biological sciences have declined from their peaks in 1973. Most of the growth has been in business and engineering (from 16 percent in 1970 to 24 percent in 1979 for business majors, and from 9 percent in 1970 to 11 percent in 1979 for engineering majors). Students appear to be moving into areas where the job market is strongest, despite the huge influx of college graduates into the labor force in recent years. Change of field choice appears to be a more prevalent adjustment to recent growth of the college cohort than does the decision not to attend college. (Most of the decline in the number of college attenders is due to a smaller total cohort rather than to a declining share of the cohort attending.)

And these adjustments seem reasonable: as more people gain college experience, the disadvantage of *not* attending becomes great, even if the relative salary advantage of the college degree has diminished. This seems particularly true when we recognize (1) that the unemployment rate for high school graduates still greatly exceeds that for college graduates; (2) much of the relative salary advantage of college graduates has been dissipated due to increases in the minimum wage and in salaries in the skilled craft industries, both of which are usually not realistic options for those deciding whether or not to attend college, and (3) the job-related benefits for minorities seem, by most evidence, to still be holding up.

Perhaps the best summary of research on the total value of a college education has been provided by Howard Bowen (1977, p. 448): "First, the monetary returns from higher education alone are probably sufficient to offset all the costs. Second, the nonmonetary returns are several times as valuable as the monetary returns. And third, the total returns from higher education in all its aspects exceed the cost by several times. In short, the cumulative evidence leaves no doubt that American higher education is well worth what it costs." Bowen's research, of course, considers much more than the job-related benefits of college, and that is as it should be. It is unfortunate that the rather simplistic, and perhaps incorrect, analyses of the job-related impacts of higher education have been interpreted by some as showing there is "too much" higher education in this country.

References

American Council on Education. *National Norms for Entering College Freshmen.* Washington, D.C.: American Council on Education, 1970–1972.

Astin, A. W. *Preventing Students from Dropping Out.* San Francisco: Jossey-Bass, 1975.

Astin, A. W. *Four Critical Years: Effects of College on Beliefs, Attitudes, and Knowledge.* San Francisco: Jossey-Bass, 1977.

Astin, A. W., and Henson, J. W. "New Measures of College Selectivity." *Research in Higher Education,* 1977, *6,* 1–9.

Astin, A. W., King., M. R., Light, J. M., and Richardson, G. T. *The American Freshmen: National Norms.* Los Angeles: University of California, 1973–1978.

Astin, A. W., King, M. R., and Richardson, G. T. *The American Freshman: National Norms.* Los Angeles: University of California, 1979.

Astin, A. W., and Panos, R. J. *The Educational and Vocational Development of American College Students.* Washington, D.C.: American Council on Education, 1969.

Astin, A. W., Panos, R. J., and Creager, J. A. *National Norms for Entering College Freshmen.* Washington, D.C.: American Council on Education, 1966–1967.

Berg, I. *Education and Jobs: The Great Training Robbery.* Boston: Beacon Press, 1971.

Bisconti, A. S. *Women: Marriage, Career, and Job Satisfaction.* Bethlehem, Pa.: The CPC Foundation, 1978.

Bisconti, A. S., and Astin, H. S. *Undergraduate and Graduate Study in Scientific Fields.* Washington, D.C.: American Council on Education, 1973.

Bisconti, A. S. and Gomberg, I. L. *The Hard-to-Place Majority—A National Study of the Career Outcomes of Liberal Arts Graduates.* Bethlehem, Pa.: The CPC Foundation, 1975.

Bisconti, A. S., and Solmon, L. C. *College Education on the Job—The Graduates' Viewpoint.* Bethlehem, Pa.: The CPC Foundation, 1976.

Bisconti, A. S., and Solmon, L. C. *Job Satisfaction After College—The Graduates' Viewpoint.* Bethlehem, Pa.: The CPC Foundation, 1977.

Bowen, H. R. *Investment in Learning: The Individual and Social Value of American Higher Education.* San Francisco: Jossey-Bass, 1977.

Creager, J. A., Astin, A. W., Boruch, R. F., and Bayer, A. E. *National Norms for Entering College Freshmen.* Washington, D.C.: American Council on Education, 1968.

Creager, J. A., Astin, A. W., Boruch, R. F., Bayer, A. E., and Drew, D. E. *National Norms for Entering College Freshmen.* Washington, D.C.: American Council on Education, 1969.

El-Khawas, E. H., and Bisconti, A. S. *Five and Ten Years After College Entry.* Washington, D.C.: American Council on Education, 1974.

Freeman, R. B. *The Market for College-Trained Manpower: A Study in the Economics of Career Choice.* Cambridge, Mass.: Harvard University Press, 1971.

Freeman, R. B. *The Over-Educated American.* New York: Academic Press, 1976.

Freeman, R. B. "The Facts About the Declining Economic Value of College." *The Journal of Human Resources,* 1980, *9* (1), 124–146.

Gordon, M. S. (Ed.). *Higher Education and the Labor Market.* New York: McGraw-Hill, 1974.

Hoyt, K. *Career Education, Vocational Education, and Occupational Education: An Approach to Defining Differences.* Columbus, Ohio: Center for Vocational Education, Ohio State University, 1974.

Mincer, J. "The Determination of Labor Incomes: A Survey with Special Reference to the Human Capital Approach." *Journal of Economic Literature,* 1970, *8,* 1–26.

O'Toole, J. "The Reserve Army of the Underemployed." *Change,* 1975, *7* (4), 26–33, 63; (5), 26–33, 60–62.

O'Toole, J. *Work, Learning, and the American Future.* San Francisco: Jossey-Bass, 1977.

Pace, C. R., and Rosenstein, C. *Seven Years Later—Education and Work: A 1977 Survey of Students Who Entered the University of California in 1970.* Los Angeles: Laboratory for Research on Higher Education, 1978.

Rumberger, R. W. "The Economic Decline of College Graduates: Fact or Fallacy?" *The Journal of Human Resources,* 1980, *15* (1), 99–112.

Schwartz, E., and Thornton, R. "Overinvestment in College Training?" *The Journal of Human Resources,* 1980, *15* (1), 77–102.

Smith, J. P., and Welch, F. "The Overeducated American? A Review Article." Discussion Paper #147. Santa Monica: The RAND Corporation, November 1978.

Solmon, L. C. "The Definition and Impact of College Quality." In L. C. Solmon and P. J. Taubman (Eds.) *Does College Matter?* New York: Academic Press, 1973.

Solmon, L. C., Bisconti, A. S., and Ochsner, N. L. *College as a Training Ground for Jobs.* New York: Praeger, 1977.

Solmon, L. C., and Hurwicz, M. L. "The Labor Market for Ph.D.s in Science and Engineering: Career Outcomes." Paper presented at annual meeting of the Eastern Economics Association, Washington, D.C., 1978.

30

Solmon, L. C., Ochsner, N. L., and Hurwica, M. L. *The Labor Market for Humanities Ph.D.'s: An Empircal Analysis.* New York: Praeger, 1979.

U.S. Bureau of the Census. *Statistical Abstract of the United States: 1976.* Washington, D.C.: U.S. Bureau of the Census, 1976.

U.S. Department of Health, Education, and Welfare. *Digest of Education Statistics: 1977-1978.* Washington, D.C.: U.S. Government Printing Office, 1978.

U.S. Department of Labor. "Job Satisfaction: Is There a Trend?" *Manpower Research Monograph,* No. 30. Washington, D.C.: U.S. Department of Labor, 1974.

U.S. Department of Labor, Bureau of Labor Statistics. "Educational Attainment of Workers." Special Labor Force Report 65. Washington, D.C.: *Monthly Labor Review,* March 1966.

U.S. Department of Labor, Bureau of Labor Statistics. "Educational Attainment of Workers." Special Labor Force Report #92. Washington, D.C.: *Monthly Labor Review,* February 1968.

U.S. Department of Labor, Bureau of Labor Statistics. "The United States Economy in 1985: An Overview of BLS Projections." Washington, D.C.: *Monthly Labor Review,* December 1973.

U.S. Department of Labor, Bureau of Labor Statistics. *Educational Attainment of Workers.* Special Labor Force Report 175. Washington, D.C.: *Monthly Labor Review,* 1975.

U.S. Department of Labor, Bureau of Labor Statistics. "Educational Attainment of Workers." Special Labor Force Report #209. Washington, D.C.: *Monthly Labor Review,* March 1978.

Witmer, D. R. "Is the Value of College Really Declining?" *Change,* 1978a, *8* (11), 46-47, 60-61.

Witmer, D. R. "Are Americans Overeducated? Are Returns on Investments in Higher Education Lower Than Those on Alternative Investments?" Paper presented at annual meeting of The American Educational Research Association, Toronto, March 1978b.

Witmer, D. R. "Has the Golden Age of American Higher Education Come to an Abrupt End?" *The Journal of Human Resources,* 1980, *15* (1), 113-120.

Lewis C. Solmon is a professor in the Graduate School of Education at UCLA and secretary treasurer of the Higher Education Research Institute. He has authored numerous works on the economics of higher education, including College Education and Employment: The Recent Graduates. *His latest book is* Adults in College.

Business and higher education look more natural as partners than as competitors.

What Business Needs from Higher Education

Donald U. Honicky

If you were to ask a sample of business representatives what business wants from higher education, a continued supply of good graduates and continued research would probably be on their lists. Some would probably say that more attention to specific skill areas such as computer programming or engineering would be helpful. Others might add that a better attitude toward government regulation or the free enterprise system would be nice.

Is There a "Business" Point of View?

In spite of the similar answers, there is not really a "business" point of view of what is needed or wanted from higher education. That is because what is often portrayed as the singular thinking of business is just the most recent pronouncement of either a very prominent business representative or an association that may represent a group of businesses. This is not to say that the thoughts or ideas are not valid or that those expressing the thoughts are not very sincere and even eager for higher education to work more closely with business. It is true, however, that most would restrict the relationship between higher education and business to the area of recruiting and financing support.

Ever so slowly, however, people are beginning to realize that there is far more to the relationship between higher education and business than just education providing the manpower and business providing the money. What is that relationship? How is it defined? How is it established?

What Is College Relations?

College relations is a subject that gets a great deal of attention without yet having been clearly defined. Perhaps the size and complexity of our institutions makes us feel that we have the time to comment on but not talk with one another. Whatever the reason for our confusion, our institutions are experiencing a growing need for mutual understanding and cooperation, and we are encountering problems in our dealings with one another because of poor or ineffective or nonexistent communication, which has resulted in misunderstandings, myths, and stereotypes.

College relations can be defined as those activities between higher education and business that are designed to improve mutual understanding and do not deal with either recruiting or the marketing of a product or service. Both business and higher education are searching for solutions to problems that plague them. These are problems that they often think are unique to their situation, but which are really shared to a greater degree than they realize. College relations deals with working together to solve mutual needs by combining mutual talents in a host of ways. Of course, there will be people in both institutions who will argue that there is enough to do without being burdened with another activity that does not seem to have much specific benefit for them.

Why College Relations?

It is hard to imagine a group of people who have a more profound effect on the business community than the students who pass through our colleges and universities and the faculty and administrators who teach and work with them. We are an educated nation that deals in ideas. For the most part, those who run our government, our educational institutions, the various media, and most special-interest groups are products of our colleges and universities. Even when this is recognized, however, there is a tendency to sidestep one another or talk "at" one another rather than taking the time to really understand. We can no longer afford to do this because there are so many similarities between our two institutions and the problems they face.

First, both business and higher education are established institutions in our society and in our communities. Both are major resources of economic and social change and mutually dependent on one another in many ways. Colleges and universities look to business for finances and for direction from business people who are on boards of trustees. Business depends on higher education for manpower and research. Moreover, since higher education provides business with innovative and creative thinkers, colleges and universities expect financial support, career guidance, and employment opportunities for their graduates.

Business and education have similar financial concerns. Increasing costs are challenging our ability to provide the public with a high-quality product. Colleges continue to face uncertain state and federal support and the constant battle of increasing costs; the direct result is an increase in tuition and fees. In business we have to raise our prices to cover increased costs, and we have the perpetual need for capitalization to cover costs of modernizing and expanding facilities. Again, the same problem is found in higher education. At the same time, both are regulated to some degree by governmental bodies. This can affect the kind of product we turn out, what it costs, and who can have it.

Of course, both institutions are faced with human-resources problems, such as housing people. On the one hand it involves dormitory space, and on the other it involves office and plant facilities. Pressures from women and minorities are having considerable effects on both colleges and corporations. There is a clear need to improve female and minority hiring and promotion.

Even the question of tenure is as important in business as it is in higher education. In both institutions it may create a group of people who are older, who are somewhat less motivated, and who perceive fewer challenges in their job. They may not want to take chances even in times of change. This is a more expensive group and may be less productive as well. Some in business may argue that this is stretching our similarities a bit, but they should look around their organizations at those who are set aside rather than being let go, at those who are known to have retired on the job because they are at a level that is seen as inviolate or because they are of an age where experience has shown the organization will keep them rather than look inhumane.

Finally, both business and higher education need to concentrate on polishing their respective public images. There is no place, however, for cosmetic treatments of real problems. Many people still feel that campuses are breeding grounds for liberalism, socialism, and the like. Professors who a few years ago would have been considered racial or extreme in their views are now finding that their views are being seriously considered; but who is to say that is not as it should be. Yet consider the questions that have been raised in recent years about corporate activities in foreign countries. What about white collar crime, environmental damage, social responsibility, and consumer problems? The public feels that both business and higher education can stand considerable improvement, whether it is true in every case or not. What is important is the public perception of the need for change.

What Does Business Need from Higher Education?

Outside of the obvious things mentioned earlier, such as good employees and good research, and the less obvious but more important need for mutual understanding, business needs a partner in fulfilling our mutual roles in society. We just do not know how to express those needs.

It is not just a question of needing more and better-trained employees. We in business need to be in a position to work with higher education to be sure that their graduates understand the changing nature of business and how they might fit into it. Moreover, though many in business say publicly that a liberal education is essential, they will nevertheless hire someone with a specific, identifiable skill like computer programming or engineering before hiring the liberal arts graduate who has a strong humanities background. For the immediate need is often to fill a specific job so that the position is productive as soon as possible.

Business needs to give more serious thought to the needs of tomorrow in our rapidly changing technological society. In so doing we need to think about more than the merely technical aspects of running a business. As New York University President John C. Sawhill said recently (1979), "The narrowly educated may know how to maximize profits, compute valences, and increase cost efficiency. But they will never know how to manage the difficult issues that we will continue to grapple with in the eighties" (p. 137).

In our anxiety to be sure that we have enough computer specialists and people with engineering or technical backgrounds, we should remember that many of our entry-level employees will some day attain positions in the higher levels of corporate management. For those positions they need to understand the way our American society has evolved from other cultures. They need an appreciation of the arts so that they can help support them. They need a sensitivity to the individual that will allow them to manage their businesses with firmness, but also with a great degree of understanding.

For business to get the kinds of people it needs (who may not be those it "wants" today), there must be a way for business and higher education to get together to consider what our two worlds are now and what we think they will become, and why. We need to bring people together in ways that encourage them to get to know one another well enough so that they start to trust one another without worrying about the trappings of their respective positions or their misconceptions about the other person.

Business also wants higher education to teach young people about our system of commerce and its relationship to the prosperity and progress in our country. Yet this does not mean that we want apologists for everything done by business or that we want people to come out of college blindly accepting what has gone on in the past without thinking about how it can be improved. There should, however, be some basic understanding of how this massive economy grinds on from month to month and year to year and why it is different from that of other nations. If college students are going to be really useful to business, they should begin intelligently understanding and questioning the economic system while they are still in the classroom. This is also a perfect time for business representatives to get themselves into the classroom discussion. There is a general hesitation to get into the liberal arts or humanities classrooms, since many business people have not understood the impact those faculty and students have on them. It should no longer continue to be so. We should recognize that these experiences can be the most interesting and valuable for all concerned.

Business is now asking that higher education pay more attention to older and nontraditional students, since they make up a greater proportion of the work force. Higher education is in a position to serve them as never before as people change careers in mid-life, or as they need to be retrained due to changing business conditions, or as more women continue to enter the work force. The kinds of training or education needed should be worked out jointly between colleges and businesses, and this requires that we establish some mechanism for dialogue.

What Are Some Specific Activities to Try?

Although there are not many models that can be cited, there are a few that might be of use. Perhaps the most significant is one developed by the Bell System and taken up and encouraged by the American Association of State Colleges and Universities (AASCU). It is called the Faculty/ Management Forum.

This program was developed by AT&T with the help of the University of Montana and Mountain Bell. It is the most basic of meeting forums designed to get the participants to know one another better in order to work together. The plan brings together six middle managers from a business and six assistant or associate professors from a college or university. The guidelines call for broad representation of departments from business and various disciplines within the college or university.

The heads of the two organizations are asked to give their blessing to letting their employees spend two and a half days talking about two very simple questions. When that agreement is given and the participants are selected, they are taken to a remote location where they will not be distracted by city life or their own offices. They are first asked to describe the characteristics of their respective institutions. They are found to be large, bureaucratic, departmentalized, stable in the community, and so forth.

Next, the participants are asked to list the concerns or problems of their institutions. Both managers and professors have financial problems, personnel concerns, consumer problems, regulatory concerns, and so forth. In fact, as the program progresses, it becomes quite evident that the roles of the individuals could be reversed and they could be describing each other's organization. When that realization strikes home they are then asked to pick the most important problems and to order them by priority. After this they are broken up into groups of four to begin talking about how they would design the approach to a solution. Not a solution, mind you, but the approach. When the meetings are over, the participants are given the charge to return to their respective organizations to continue working together in groups of four to better define the approaches they have identified.

In the process of working together over a month or two, the participants start to know one another better and in many cases they become close friends. They come to understand how busy the others are and what their problems are. In addition, they start to find ways of using each other's talents in their own work. For example, professors will invite their business partners into the classrooms to talk about their jobs; business participants will have the professors into the office to help study a problem or consult on an activity. Without knowing it, they have begun a whole series of activities that cement relations and really improve understanding. These activities constitute the sort of collaboration called for by A. Bartlett Giamatti (1978), president of Yale University, in his inaugural address: "The ancient ballet of mutual antagonism . . . between private enterprise . . . and . . . education . . . is not to anyone's interest. That ballet of antagonism must give way to a capacity for responsible collaboration."

The AASCU has encouraged the continuation and expansion of this process. It has been used at Winthrop College in Rock Hill, South Carolina, at Marshall University in Huntington, West Virginia, at the State University of New York at Albany, and at West Liberty State College in West Virginia. Companies such as Ashland Oil, Springs Mills, New York Telephone, Huntington Alloys, Fostoria Glass, and the Chesapeake and Potomac Telephone Company of West Virginia have taken part, and more programs are being planned at Marshall University and Winthrop College. It is a simple process that costs little to initiate, but the results are astounding. In fact, the secret is the simplicity, since there is no attention given to formality, dress, titles, plush accommodations, and so forth. Since the accent is on talking with one another about what we share in characteristics and concerns, we find that the people cannot help but work together.

A second innovation of substantial promise has been the classroom game-simulations designed with the assistance of AT&T for use in a number of disciplines. They are simple to play because they are not computer-based or intricate in design and take only about an hour to play (so that they fit into an average classroom period). Moreover, they deal with subjects that are of current interest and create realistic situations for discussion. The subjects are ethics (Where Do You Draw the Line?); privacy (The Privacy Game); corporate social responsibility (Relocation: A Corporate Decision), and utility economics (Trebedies Island).

It Can Be Done

Regardless of who is involved or the strategy for creating mutual involvement, the key to business and higher education getting what they need is simplicity and honesty. The more candid we are with one another and the more we stay away from complexity of program design, the more time we have to really get to know and understand the other person. There are a lot of practical things we can do that do not take a lot of time or money. We have to strive for communication on matters of substance rather than those of form, and—above all—we must be prepared to go out of our way in order to really understand one another.

Reference

"Interview with John C. Sawhill." *The New York Post*, January 16, 1979, p. 137.

Donald U. Honicky is division manager of community relations for AT&T. Among his contributions to higher education was his development of the Faculty-Management Forum and the coauthorship of a series of classroom game-simulations about the problems of modern business. He has been active with many associations of higher education and frequently addresses various meetings on the subject of improving understanding between business and higher education.

*Colleges and universities can creatively respond
to the interests and needs of the business
community and affirm the importance of the liberal
arts while doing so.*

What Higher Education
Has to Offer Business

Alberta Arthurs

There are some clear answers to the question, What does business have to offer higher education? Those of us in colleges and universities know that we need the contributions of business for new academic programs; we need the matching funds, the employee tuition plans, and the scholarship programs that business offers. We need entry-level jobs for our graduates. We need the expertise of business for our boards of trustees and for our own internal management strategies. We need the support of business, both within our communities and at the national level. The parallel question, What does higher education have to offer business?, has less obvious answers, although educators find themselves pondering it these days, and liberal arts educators ponder it most wonderingly.

At Chatham College, we have thought about the relationship of business and higher education a great deal, somewhat to our own surprise. A small college for women, 112 years old, Chatham has a wooded campus, dotted with mansions, small gardens, and walks. There is a chapel in the center of the campus, crystal chandeliers in the music building, leaded-glass windows, and ivy everywhere. Hidden among hills and hollows, Chatham has been known for a century as the little jewel or the gem of the city of Pittsburgh. It is a college with a dedicated faculty, a strong library, a demanding program for educating its students: a classic liberal arts institution. Like other liberal arts institutions, the college has historically had little to share with the commercial world beyond it.

But Chatham, surrounded as it is by hills and homes, is also surrounded by a great number of very large, Pittsburgh-based corporations and the smaller businesses, agencies, and arts organizations that the corporations spawn and support. In recent years, Chatham and the larger community have begun to acknowledge each other in programs that are indicative of the new links possible between colleges and corporations. All these programs involve both corporate employees and members of the college's academic departments; all have demanded fresh energy and ideas at the college; all have met with enthusiastic acceptance by business, although only after careful preparation and consistent presentation by us; and all are intended to meet the needs of business *and* the college.

In the chapter "Careers, Curricula, and the Future of the Liberal Arts" in this volume, four thoughtful teachers make a case for tradition and for change. The liberal learning tradition, and specifically the discipline of sociology, is to be preserved through change, in the plan of action proposed. The changes—all supplementary to the study of sociology—are meant to enhance that study through practical application and career-counseling opportunities. In its relationship to the business community that surrounds it, Chatham has taken a stand similar to that which has developed in that imaginative sociology department. Most significantly, as this chapter will attempt to show, the purpose of our cooperative efforts with business is identical; that is, to sustain and strengthen liberal education.

There are at least five ways in which this college has initiated interaction with business. First, in recent years, the college has adopted some nontraditional course offerings. There are courses at Chatham in management, statistics, communications, computer science, and accounting, all immensely popular areas of study. These course offerings are set within the liberal arts framework and are dependent on that framework. Students who study management, for example, are required to take courses in several other, more traditional areas of the college curriculum. Computer science students must major in a traditional discipline. Like many other colleges, we continue to experiment with a good mix and balance of liberal arts and those preprofessional courses we make available.

Second, our internship program, also like those at other institutions, has established immensely successful ties between the business community and the college. Taken for credit under supervision of both a faculty member at the college and a professional on the job, internships make education more specific and useful both to the student and to business. The political science major interning in sales at Westinghouse Electric Corporation, an English major working in contract negotiations at U.S. Steel, or a language major doing translations at Mellon Bank see a side of their study they might not otherwise see. Almost all our students currently undertake at least one internship before graduation. Consequently, we have greatly expanded our career-planning and job-placement activities. In the last four years, the number of corporate recruiters on campus in the spring has tripled.

Third, and most recently, we have established special career-development programs for local corporations. In 1979, the college and the Human Resources Division of the Gulf Oil Corporation mounted a Career Development Program for women employees of Gulf. Career-planning sessions, personal assessment and testing, special advising, lectures, and workshops were designed for the selected participants. Faculty members from Chatham College were heavily involved in the project, helping the Gulf women plan career and educational goals. Similar programs have since been mounted for other corporations, both in and outside of Pittsburgh.

Fourth, conferences and non-credit courses at the college focus on the increasingly prominent role of women in business. The college has sponsored a conference for women directors and trustees, courses on money management for women, and workshops in estate planning, self-employment, and tax strategies. A recent conference on Men and Women in the Corporation was aimed at area chief executive officers and human-resource professionals. With the support of the National Science Foundation, we offer a program designed to return women college graduates to work in industrial chemistry. With a grant from the IBM Corporation, we offer a summer program in business essentials for liberal arts graduates.

Finally, the college clearly takes corporate needs and interests very seriously. As an educational institution, we strive to run well an organization in which the kind of people we graduate are in charge. The college publishes an annual report; we run our finances by rules of the industrial world; we use corporate standards to measure our management achievements; we try to involve our faculty and students in decision making. We try not to make excuses for ourselves because we are an educational institution; we try instead to provide a model of good administration. As a college, we consider it an obligation to make it clear that we—as educators, especially as educators of women—understand the realities of the business world.

There are still a great many projects that we must undertake. For instance, we should make a more concentrated and consistent effort to use businessmen and women in our classes and extracurricular activities. We have some visitors now, but we need to make a larger effort to use the expertise that surrounds us. We would like to make a greater effort to find internships and research sabbaticals in industry for our faculty. We would like to collaborate with Pittsburgh corporations in the collection of data on the careers of liberal arts graduates in corporations and of women in corporations. We would like to find more ways to help corporations advance women, and we are concerned about bettering the educational programs available for working people.

Chatham, and colleges like it, are dealing with such problems for a variety of reasons. Obviously, we have a need to attract new populations and new sources of support. These innovative programs help us to do that. But more importantly, we feel the need to defend the role of higher education in society, and especially the role of the liberal arts. Working with business is one very important way in which we can impress society with the solutions that liberal arts practitioners can supply to the mighty problems we face.

If colleges and universities do *not* make the case for the liberal arts in the 1980s, we must expect the liberal arts to fail. If we do not claim the attention of the society around us, we will forfeit the attention of the society around us. Without insisting on the meaningfulness of the humanities, we lose that meaningfulness. Education cannot hide among the hills and hollows and libraries of academe; so, at Chatham, we have entered the work spaces, the computer centers, and even the board rooms of the corporate community that surrounds us.

But is that all? Are such programs enough? As interesting as these kinds of adventures are, a fundamental challenge still remains. Is the appropriate response of higher education to business merely the supplying of programs and services, a kind of creative "me-too"? Is it the task of liberal arts educators simply to recognize such needs and to meet them? Should we be satisfied with such adaptations in education as have been described here?

The answer to each of those questions is, obviously, "no." Ultimately, what higher education offers society, including business, is research, reason, and informed intelligence, the discipline of close reading and of examined experience. The liberal arts offers business analytic abilities, developed imagination, and abilities to measure, judge, assess, and free ideas from their contexts, and to generate new ideas. The liberal arts offers society hope of overcoming that which is narrow, specialized, mechanical, automatic, or ordinary. The liberal arts has always interpreted society as it was being built. The function of the liberal arts is no different today, and it is as urgent as ever.

A small "case study" in the true applicability of education to the world of business would be helpful here. During one of our seminars last year, some students worked on Sir Thomas Malory's *Morte d'Arthur,* the fifteenth-century English narrative version of the King Arthur material. We focused on the final two books of this work, in which Malory retells the story of Lancelot and Guinevere, the story of the fall of the Round Table and all it stood for, "The fairest fellowship of noble knights that ever held Christian kings together." In these dramatic chapters of the legendary material, the students made some interesting discoveries in literary parallelism, such as the following examples:

1. A scene in which Lancelot and Guinevere are almost found bedded together by their enemies. In a later, critical scene, they *are* found bedded together, and the kingdom begins to collapse.
2. Scenes of the heroic tournaments for play, in which knights of the Round Table pitted themselves against each other in mock battle. Such scenes serve to tragically pre-figure the true battle-ground, later in the work, in which Arthur's forces fight Lancelot's forces in real battle and all the knights are doomed.
3. An early episode in which Lancelot rescues Guinevere, with ease, from a cowardly villain. Later he must rescue her, with pain and tragic consequences, from a fiery death at the hands of Arthur himself.
4. Scenes in which Lancelot and Guinevere make small lies, half-truths, excuses and denials as lovers, and as Arthur's friends. These understandable deceptions that are meant to preserve the kingdom mount in intensity until the two are telling great, direct lies.
5. Two scenes of "lusty" May. In the first, May "flowereth and flourisheth" in beauty and in joy. In the second, there is "a great anger and unhappiness."

The students found many more such instances of dramatic parallelism and foreshadowing in the work. They were being clever readers and good literary critics, discovering techniques of dramatic art, devices by which this fifteenth-century author builds his characters and portrays the mores of a fictional society.

These would have been perfectly good discoveries if the students had stopped at that, but they did not. They also discovered that these echoes and anticipations of the final tragedy demonstrate the inevitability of that tragedy. They learned that the scenes illustrate the philosophical and political reverberations of pretense and hypocrisy. Even when initiated in the name of love and friendship, such reverberations are more than the society can withstand. Such parallelism showed forth the inevitability of disaster, even the progress toward it, when there are lies, and, through those lies, repeated damage to the standards of society. The students discovered through these parallelisms that passions, unrestrained and unchallenged, repeat and intensify and finally destroy. It is the passionate attachment of Guinevere and Lancelot, the passionate hatred of their enemies, even the passionate ambition of the good king, that are played out over and over in these paralleled scenes. Unexamined and unchecked, the passions accelerate into tragedy and into the death of a society. Private passions finally outweigh public purposes, and irrationality reigns in Arthur's kingdom.

The students were engaged in the following: the intelligent reading of difficult material, the analysis of human motivation and movement, and the recognition of patterns and order, and of the forces that can disturb or transform them. The students raised questions about the nature of an institution and of the individual within an institution. They explored the great moral issues surrounding loyalty, honor, and the workings of society. They discussed the vision of perfection as exemplified in the Round Table, and the irony of the tragic end of that vision. They also discussed the enduring fascination of that vision of perfection.

Such questions as these, and the ability to raise and analyze them, are critical to business. Indeed, they are critical to American society at large. It is our obligation as citizens to understand the forces, ambitions, passions, and visions that generate success and failure. Business, it seems clear, is far better off if higher education can continue to offer not merely conferences, internships, career counseling, and preprofessional courses, but such discourse and discoveries as those students undertook in their study of Malory. Such discourse and discussions are—most importantly and finally—what higher education has to offer business.

Alberta Arthurs is professor of English and president of Chatham College in Pittsburgh, Pennsylvania. She has taught and held administrative positions at Tufts, Rutgers, and Harvard Universities, and she is a frequent speaker on subjects related to higher education and literature.

The role of the arts in liberal education is to unlock a treasure-house of insights and perceptions into our lives and times.

The Visual Arts and Liberal Education: Not Yet a Marriage

Clinton Adams

It is not yet a marriage: The arts and liberal education share a living arrangement at best. They are roommates within the university, an odd couple whose relationship is characterized by constant tensions and misunderstandings. As in most such misunderstandings, there are causes on both sides.

In part, tensions exist because of the character of the visual arts; in part they exist because of the relatively recent arrival of the artist within the university. During most of the nineteenth century, the education of the artist in the United States was centered in independent academies and art schools that closely resembled their European models and were located in the principal cities of the east and midwest—Boston, New York, Philadelphia, Cincinnati, and Chicago. Only late in the century were the first art departments established within the universities (Yale in 1869, Syracuse in 1873). Most American artists still received their training in the art academies in the early twentieth century, often combining their study in the United States with a year or more in Europe.

The expansion of the visual arts within the universities was not without opposition. Liberal education, as administered by the faculties of colleges of arts and sciences, has a difficult time with fields that are neither verbal nor quantitative in character. The creative process of artists is perceived to be essentially irrational; by definition, its outcome cannot be predicted, and the works that artists produce are not susceptible to either objective appraisal or quantifiable measurement of their value. Professors in the traditional academic disciplines, while perhaps intrigued by the arts, often retain a puritanical distrust of the makers of "graven images." They remember that Plato excluded the visual artist from the republic. They recall with little enthusiasm the art education to which they were subjected in the public schools, and in so doing tend to lump their colleagues in the fine arts together with those in education, not ordinarily a group held in high esteem. They are uncomfortable with the seemingly eccentric character of modern art (Wald, 1956).

It is natural in these circumstances that within many universities the study of the history of art was accepted far more readily than was the practice of art (Ritchie, 1966). Art history, though late in establishment, is in every sense an academic discipline; its methods are closely related to those of other fields within the humanities, and its faculties are qualified as scholars. The practice of art, however, entered most universities through the back door; it began either in teacher-training programs or in a few practical courses, such as perspective and drafting, which might be of use to architects or scientists. The early studio faculties were generally limited to those who held proper academic credentials, which meant, for the most part, men and women who had completed their graduate study in the teachers' colleges. Emphasis in the teacher-training programs was often placed upon design and the handcrafts rather than upon painting and sculpture, further adding to a suspicion that their character might not be truly appropriate for inclusion within the university.

The very substantial growth of art studio programs, usually within separate schools or colleges of fine arts, has occurred after World War II. With the financial aid of the federal government, large numbers of veterans came to the campuses. There was an air of ferment and excitement, and in no field was this greater than in the visual arts. In part, this excitement was a reflection of a vigorous new spirit in American art, although, paradoxically, the very character of that art has brought about new suspicion and, on occasion, hostility within the universities. The intellectual and conceptual character of modernist and postmodernist art is neither fully perceived nor much liked by conservative academicians, whose personal tastes have been formed at best by realism and impressionism and at worst by commercial illustration. These attitudes exist despite the fact that the universities now exert an overwhelming influence upon professional education in the arts. A large proportion of America's most distinguished creative artists hold faculty appointments. An increasing proportion of younger artists receive their professional training in the universities rather than in the academies. Because the universities are themselves geographically dispersed, artists now live and work in every section of the country. One result has been to engender new levels of quality in exhibitions at regional museums and a new awareness of art upon the part of the public that lives outside the older metropolitan areas. But although the universities have enjoyed remarkable growth in their professional programs (and in so doing have altered, for better or for worse, the character of American painting, printmaking, and sculpture), the uneasy relationship between the visual arts and liberal education remains largely unresolved.

University professors tend in academic matters to accept change with great reluctance; art and the artist remain strangers in their midst. And while course requirements and curricula vary from institution to institution, they are more alike than different, and the content of liberal education is determined primarily within colleges of arts and sciences. Some kind of balance exists among requirements in English, the humanities, the social and natural sciences, mathematics, and foreign languages. Seldom is there a specific requirement in the visual arts; seldom is the question even raised. The result is that very large numbers of students preparing for careers as scientists, engineers, business executives, lawyers, and medical doctors graduate from the university with little or no experience of or information about the arts. And few even seem to care.

The fault lies not only with the arts and sciences faculties. Within colleges of fine arts, few of the artist-teachers who constitute the studio faculties are deeply concerned about liberal education. Most of their energies, as is the case in other professional fields, are centered on courses for advanced undergraduate and graduate students who seek to enter careers in the arts. All too often these artist-teachers are themselves lacking in the perspectives that a liberal education provides.

Does it matter that students graduating from universities are less familiar with Michelangelo than with Shakespeare, or with Rembrandt than with Copernicus? Certainly it does, because in the absence of such information Western civilization is gradually eroded and diminished. The insights of the great artists of the past are no less relevant and valuable today than are those of writers, poets, historians, and scientists of the past. But beyond such information, something else is lacking when students fail to gain a genuine understanding of the visual arts as an intrinsic component of liberal education. They fail to gain access to a presentational "language" that is capable of conveying meanings quite different from those that are conveyed in written or mathematical form (Langer, 1957).

The perceptions and conceptions of artists are *presented* in their work. We should not be misled by the fact that painting and sculpture are presentational rather than discursive, or by the fact that the meanings presented are non-verbal rather than verbal. Art deals with ideas. The ideas are of a different kind from the ideas presented in verbal disciplines, and further dimensions are added to the human mind by encountering and perceiving them. In Leo Steinberg's phrase, "the eye is a part of the mind"

(1953). Great works of art provide insight into life, love and death, comedy and tragedy—every aspect of human existence. The genius of great artists lies not in their technical skills but in the depth of their perceptions and in their ability to discover forms through which these perceptions may be visually presented.

The visual arts lend themselves to the widely prevalent misconception that because a work of art can be seen in an instant, it can be quickly or instantly apprehended. This is not the case; it has never been the case. For example, even the relatively accessible naturalistic landscapes of the nineteenth century require for their full apprehension that the viewer come to them with perceptions formed both through experience of the art that preceded them and through knowledge of the counter-currents of classicism and romanticism that swirled back and forth throughout that century. The remarkable diversity that is a principal characteristic of avant-garde art in the twentieth century creates a situation far more complex. The art of this century is exceedingly rich; it is capable of providing important insights into the nature of the difficult times in which we live, but it can be perceived only partially and inadequately in the absence of an understanding of the intricate sociological, political, and cultural forces that brought the avant-garde into being (Poggioli, 1968). The role of the arts in liberal education is to provide the key that will unlock a treasure-house of insights and perceptions into our lives and times. Because such perceptions are so deeply needed by all those who will follow careers in business, politics, and the sciences, failure to include the arts as a central component of liberal learning is a critical omission.

Ideally, experience of the arts should include direct, hands-on experience in addition to visual, critical, and historical study. The act of drawing educates the eye and the mind even more than it educates the hand; the experience of gazing attentively at a model, be it a person or a tree, and endeavoring to record what one sees is a first step toward the discovery that to make a meaningful drawing, one must see and record *selectively*. This fact, even today, provides the scientific illustrator with an advantage over the technically perfect but unselective vision of the camera. But comprehension of the language of vision, like other languages, is not innate; it must be acquired through study and hard work.

The declining verbal literacy of entering college students has been the subject of countless articles. Equal concern has been expressed about deteriorating mathematical abilities. Yet little has been said about the low level of visual awareness that pervades American society. Despite a growing interest in preservation of the environment, the country as a whole appears willing to tolerate the visual blight created by urban jungles of signs, utility poles, weeds, junked automobiles, and ever-present litter. Nor is the mess in which we live confined to the cities. Throughout the nation's most scenic areas it becomes increasingly difficult to find vistas unspoiled by billboards, clutter, smog, and debris.

Neither the decline in literacy nor the lack of visual awareness arises from a single cause; both have complex roots in society and education. No panaceas exist through which either may be overcome. In the case of the visual arts, the first necessary (but not sufficient) step is to achieve recognition of the problem within the universities. It is essential to perceive the arts not as a frill or eccentricity, but rather as an intrinsic part of liberal learning, and not as an enemy of the intellect (Barzun, 1959), but as one of its components, without which the fabric of western civilization is impoverished and incomplete. Only in this way can the still uneasy relationship between the arts and liberal education be resolved and the marriage consummated at last.

References

Barzun, J. *The House of Intellect*. New York: Harper & Row, 1959.

Kerr, C. "The Carnegie Commission Looks at the Arts." Paper presented at a meeting of the International Council of Fine Arts Deans, Atlanta, October 19, 1973.

Langer, S. K. *Philosophy in a New Key*. (3rd Ed.) Cambridge, Mass.: Harvard University Press, 1957.

Mills, F. V., McCulley, C., and Maddox, D. *The Status of the Visual Arts in Higher Education*. Normal, Ill.: National Council of Art Administrators, 1976.

Morrison, J. *The Rise of the Arts on the American Campus*. New York: McGraw-Hill, 1973.

Poggioli, R. *The Theory of the Avant-Garde*. Cambridge, Mass.: Harvard University Press, 1968.

Ritchie, A. C. *The Visual Arts in Higher Education*. New Haven, Conn.: College Art Association, 1966.

Steinberg, L. "The Eye is a Part of the Mind." In S. Langer (Ed.), *Reflections on Art*. Baltimore: Johns Hopkins University Press, 1958.

Wald, G. "The Artist in the University." In *The Report of the Committee on the Visual Arts at Harvard University*. Cambridge, Mass.: Harvard University Press, 1956.

Clinton Adams is an artist and art historian.
Author of numerous books and articles on
lithography, he is professor of art and director
of Tamarind Institute at the University of New
Mexico, where for fifteen years (1961–1976) he
was dean of the University's College of Fine Arts.
During this time he also served a term as president of
the International Council of Fine Arts Deans.

*Black studies has had as difficult a time
defining its boundaries and establishing its
legitimacy, as have other disciplines descendant
from philosophy. A new curriculum is designed to
fulfill the promise of black studies.*

The Coming of Age of Black Studies: Beyond "Relevance"

Vivian V. Gordon

The Beginnings

Black studies was established as an academic discipline on white university campuses in the late 1950s and early 1960s in the midst of the student protest movements of that era. In protesting, these students were seeking to redress the failure of the universities to deal with the many pressing social problems of the day, in particular, the dominant issues of war and peace and socioeconomic inequality. Universities were thus viewed by students as "ivory towers," unconcerned with translating theory or research into policies relevant to the lives of ordinary individuals in American society.

While sharing the concerns of white students, black students also protested the traditional, Eurocentric foci of American higher education. They spoke about the lack of relevance of their courses to the minority experience and the absence of academic attention to research about the experience of the black minority. The protesting black students emphasized that a few courses that considered Negro history, or selected categories of black music or black writers, were not a sufficient commitment to the study of the black experience.

Many universities yielded to the demands of protesting students, often after serious on-campus conflict, and they initiated black studies to which there was not a genuine academic commitment. In many instances, black studies programs were hastily developed, and hence little thought was given to long-range financial or faculty support. All too often the black studies programs were designed to fail or, at best, were expected to have limited academic impact.

There were failures even where black students themselves were deeply involved in creating new programs. Most students were not aware of the kinds of academic underpinnings necessary for a valid new discipline to sustain itself and flourish. Moreover, many of the most active and capable students became victims of the programs they initiated. They often pursued a poorly planned, often unorganized and nondirected course of study, which touched on popular black concerns but made little contribution to the development of those academic skills needed for either the perceptive appreciation or the critical evaluation of the world around them. Consequently, many black studies programs came to be viewed by both black and white students and faculty as rhetorical therapy sessions rather than programs of serious academic intent.

In summary, the problems that confronted black studies in those earliest days were many. But it must be emphasized that it was against overwhelming odds, often within very hostile environments, that black studies was initiated and then challenged to develop and prove its intellectual validity. For black studies this continues to be the challenge (Record, 1974).

The young people who were in the forefront of the activities leading to the establishment of black studies programs were students of courage and commitment. Clearly, they were students who placed a special value upon the concept of education for service. In so doing they reflected the historic call to blacks in higher education for leadership—the call to be the scholar/activist. Such students were reading, discussing, and responding to the mandate that emerged from works of black scholars, such as DuBois, Frazier, and Cruse, to name only a few.

Thus an important part of the promise of black studies is the ongoing resilience and resourcefulness of the black students. These are the students who pursue black studies today in a continuous search for information about the range of the Afro-American contributions to the development of America and western society. The inquiring minds of today's students are the catalysts that contribute to the dynamic of black studies. Such students are fully in agreement with the statement that black studies is ripe with the stuff of intellectual creativity.

The New Discipline: Emergence and Definition

We have given emphasis to the protest conditions under which programs of black studies emerged on the campuses of most white colleges and universities. In so doing we risk exaggerating the uniqueness of black studies. It is therefore appropriate that we also emphasize that this struggle for emergence and recognition is a process with many historical precedents.

First, all new disciplines have faced a lengthy and difficult adolescent period in which they detached themselves from an academic parent reluctant not only to let go but also to accord legitimacy to its offspring (Bierstedt, 1974, p. 4). It is hardly surprising, then, that black studies has had to share with disciplines that gained autonomy and recognition earlier than black studies the charges that it was a fad, merely trendy, or even pseudointellectual (Adams, 1980). As Cruse (1979, p. 87) has noted, "It will take many generations of students and teachers to develop Afro-American studies to the level of a traditional discipline. Afro-American studies is going to demand a high order of intellectual creativity."

Second, we cannot fully understand the emergence of the field of black studies without considering the research on the black experience undertaken over many years at predominantly black institutions. Such schools have historically given extensive attention to the works of black scholars, many of whom were among their distinguished faculty. Most graduates of southern black institutions are familiar with the works of such scholars as W.E.B. DuBois, Charles S. Johnson, Carter G. Woodson, Luther P. Jackson, James High Johnston, E. Franklin Frazier, James Weldon Johnson, Sterling Brown, J. Saunders Redding, John Hope Franklin, Horace Cayton, Horace Mann Bond, and St. Clair Drake. These scholars, who persisted in their research about the Afro-American experience in a time when such research went unheralded, developed the body of information upon which contemporary black studies programs are founded.

The tradition established by these black scholars provides today's black studies scholars with a mandate to continue to report and record cultural experience and to develop those new paradigms or models for the analysis of the Afro-American experience that often challenge the conventional wisdom.

Now that we have considered the historical conditions under which black studies has emerged, we may now define black studies as the analysis of the conditions that have affected the economic, psychological, legal, and moral status of the African in America as well as in the African diaspora. Not only is black studies concerned with the culture of the Afro-American ethnic as historically and sociologically defined by the traditional literature, but it is also concerned with the development of new approaches to the study of the black experience and of social policies that will positively affect the lives of black people.

Although we have proposed a definition of black studies, it is imprecise and will remain so for the foreseeable future. The boundaries of the discipline are subject to dispute, just as they are in other disciplines, in terms of both theoretical and methodological approaches. Consider, for example, the social science disciplines. In economics, we speak of the Keynesian school, the neo-Marxist school, and the neo-classical economics of Milton Friedman. Similarly, there are those who consider social psychology to be misplaced if taught in sociology programs, while others would consider the subject misplaced if taught in psychology programs. Fortunately, American higher education has tolerated such diversity within most of its disciplines. We hope the same courtesy will be extended in the future to black studies, which continues to be burdened by demands for exact definitions.

Black Studies in the 1980s

Given the present economic position of the nation, and of black Americans in particular, black college students preparing to enter the job market and the "American mainstream" may anticipate problems when they hold credentials reflecting specialized study in so-called "soft areas," such as sociology, history, English, philosophy, and psychology. An increasingly technological society demands an increasingly more educated employee; the B.A. degree has become only the first of a required list of credentials. Clearly, the current employment outlook mandates that an increased proportion of black college students plan for graduate or professional study.

Moreover, the undergraduate curriculum of black studies must help the student develop skills that are important to a critical analysis of both the past and present and to the factors that will affect the life of black people in America. Such curriculum must broadly prepare the student, as does a more conventional liberal arts curriculum, for graduate study as well as for postcollege employment in a range of areas. The structure of the curriculum must also allow for specialized courses that will focus upon topics of concern to students, with specific applied and pre-professional goals in mind.

The model black studies curriculum recently adopted for inclusion in the accreditation recommendations of the National Council on Black Studies (1979) seeks to fulfill all these goals. The model curriculum specifies four levels of courses. The first level consists of a single course, Introduction to Black Studies. The second level consists of introductory core courses in three broad areas: (1) the social and behavioral sciences (for example, Social Movements, Race Relations); (2) history (for example, African Pre-History, Afro-American History Through the Reconstruction Era); (3) cultural studies (for example, art, music, aesthetics). Level three consists of more advanced courses in these same three broad areas. The fourth level consists of a senior seminar, a capstone course for the students' programs of study.

It might be wise to add a unit on research methods to the model because black students need to develop a mastery of basic research skills in these times of complex and often quantitative, computer-based research. Where possible, not only should the fundamentals of the various research methodologies be taught, but students should also be directed in the reading of the best examples of research using such methodologies.

Too often the Afro-American ethnic community is viewed as a homogenous one. Perhaps this view prevails because of the common historic experience of oppression. In any case, black studies is founded upon a recognition of the diversity of the Afro-Americans and the diversity of their experiences (Cruse, 1979). As the previous discussion implies, the black studies curriculum recognizes the diversity of the black community and the right of the individual to choose the place and the manner of participating in that community. The importance of black studies as a part of the course agenda remains, regardless of the student's educational goal—whether it be for a predominantly vocational program, a broad-based, liberal arts program, or some combination of these (Carter, 1980).

Black Studies for All Students

To suggest that black studies is only for black students is to set absurd limits upon a discipline with unlimited potential. All students should be encouraged to participate in black studies programs because an understanding of the black experience is imperative in a nation where the Afro-American constitutes a significant minority and there is an increased emphasis upon a united but culturally diversified people.

References

Adams, R. L. "Evaluating Professionalism in the Context of Afro-American Studies." *The Western Journal of Black Studies*, 1980, *4* (2), 140–147.

Bierstedt, R. *The Social Order.* New York: McGraw-Hill, 1974.

Carter, H. M. "The Functional Significance of Higher Education for Black Students." *The Western Journal of Black Studies*, 1980, *4* (2), 57–65.

Cruse, H. "The Academic Side of the Movement and the Movement Side of the Academic." In V. V. Gordon (Ed.), *Lectures: Black Scholars on Black Issues.* Washington, D.C.: University Press of America, 1979.

National Council on Black Studies. "Report of the Curriculum Committee." Bloomington: Indiana University, 1979.

Record, W. "Response of Sociologists to Black Studies." In J. E. Blackwell and M. Janowitz (Eds.), *Black Sociologists: Historical and Contemporary Perspectives.* Chicago: University of Chicago Press, 1974.

Vivian V. Gordon is associate professor of sociology and former director of the African and Afro-American Studies Program at the University of Virginia. Her current research is a historical and sociological analysis of the black community in Muncie, Indiana, the town first immortalized by the Lynds' Middletown *and* Middletown in Transition.

*Applications to the Division of Education Programs
of the National Endowment for the Humanities offer
evidence for some optimism about the next decade.
The heart of that optimism is that faculty are
planning to help themselves and are not looking
for a miraculous solution.*

The Liberal Arts and the Federal Government

Geoffrey Marshall

What do we know about the 1980s that will have an effect on the teaching of the humanities? We know that the number of eighteen-year-olds in the population will decline approximately 20 percent by 1990 (Chronicle of Higher Education, 1980); we know that the student body will be older, perhaps approaching an average age of twenty-eight to thirty; and we know that these older students will be less mobile, partly because more of them will be working and partly because of the cost of transportation.

We also know that there will be painful discussions about the proper relationship of public and private education, discussions that will be intimately tied to another issue of unknown dimensions for the coming decade—the rate of inflation. The public-private issue is graphically represented in just one statistic: the tuition for a medical student at Georgetown University in 1980 was more than $14,000 a year, whereas the tuition for a medical student in the University of Texas system was less than $750 a year.

The typical triad of undergraduate course groupings—general education, major, and electives—has, for large numbers of students, been reduced to just two groupings: a shrinking number of general education courses and a growing batch of major or major-related courses. The flexibility and breadth intended by elective hours has turned, ironically, into an opportunity for students to further narrow their studies.

We know less explicitly, but much more profoundly or emotionally, that there is a broad, even ubiquitous sense of having lost our education foundations, of having lost principles that made educational decisions possible. There is a widespread sense that we have lost a national consensus about the nature and purposes of education. (We are experiencing the sense of loss and of anomie even though such a consensus may not have existed.)

What will be described now is how institutions have recently responded to these circumstances—*if* one were to judge by applications to the Division of Education Programs at the National Endowment for the Humanities (NEH). This is NEH's and the federal government's source of support for the development of curriculum, of curriculum materials, and related faculty development in the humanities. It is within this division that one would expect to find the best evidence of institutional response to changing circumstances. What does one find by examining recent applications? Two findings dominate all others. First, faculty have left the structure and content of the major untouched and, second, there has been an enormous and imaginative effort to reexamine and reshape the role of the humanities in general education and in the education of non-majors.

It is not certain why there are not many efforts to revise the major, but perhaps most faculty in history, literature, and philosophy attribute the decline in enrollments and majors to economic circumstances that are external to their courses, their departments, and even their colleges and universities. The reasons for the decline cannot be traced to the Shakespeare requirement or the senior historiography seminar, and no amount of redesign will arrest vocational flight.

But once this has been said, the next step is to recognize that there have been a great many other kinds of applications to NEH, and many of them reveal growth, excitement, and purpose on the part of planners and their colleagues. It may be that the roots of many of these applications are in economic conditions—probably so. Whatever the motivating forces, faculty have used the past few years to undertake some of the most significant and influential self-examinations in the history of American education. These self-examinations are in three areas: (1) general education requirements, (2) new majors or new areas of concentration, and (3) continuing education.

General Education

The national reexamination of general education is heavily documented. The result of this renewed interest in the nature of general education has been an almost universal reaffirmation of the centrality of the liberal arts.

In a related development, departments have, with various degrees of reluctance, abandoned the notion that the freshman is, in each and every instance, a potential Ph.D. Whatever the steps are in the march toward the doctorate, such steps are widely assumed nowadays not to begin for every student in the freshman and sophomore years. Similarly, faculty have given renewed attention to the efficacy of interdisciplinary courses in the general education requirements and in core courses. The most common form of the interdisciplinary program is general education course work arranged by theme: "The Hero," "Three Civilizations," "The Human Condition."

New Areas of Effort

Interdisciplinary work can also take the form of complex new programs, from the growth and flourishing of women's studies throughout the nation to the geographically specific Great Plains Studies at Emporia State University and the Southern Culture program at the University of Mississippi. Indeed, there is one interdisciplinary subject that seems to fly in the face of the gloom of current statistics, and that is "legal studies." NEH has helped the development of several legal studies programs (for example, at Rice University and at the University of Massachusetts/Boston) and has discovered widespread interest in the subject. One hundred institutions attended a legal studies conference in the fall of 1979 at Rice, for example, with only half that number receiving external support for attending the conference. A side-effect of implementing legal studies programs has been the growth, even the doubling, of philosophy majors, as students take a legal studies course and discover that what interests them is not the law but the interplay of philosophic ideas.

If the result of reexamination of the general education curriculum has often been interdisciplinary work, examination of the relationships of humanities departments to the rest of the college or university has resulted in the establishment of much stronger ties to pre-professional education. NEH has had a major impact on the development of humanities courses as part of the medical curriculum in this country, and has also helped a number of schools develop pre-professional humanities courses for students intending careers in medicine, business, and engineering.

More generally, we have seen many applications designed to modify existing courses or to develop new ones that will internationalize the curriculum or reflect the cultural pluralism of this nation. Internationalizing the curriculum is reflected most vividly in applications that include the world of Islam and those that incorporate the cultures, history, and politics of Asia.

Cultural pluralism is also reflected in the integration into the curriculum of substantial and sophisticated information about American blacks, as well as in some spottier efforts to do the same for the

Spanish-speaking cultures and even a recent immigrant group, the Vietnamese.

Continuing Education

Finally, faculty are slowly beginning to look at continuing education, a form of higher education whose condition can be described by noting that there are a number of colleges in this country in which departments will not accept continuing education courses toward the completion of degrees, even though the courses were designed and are taught by the same faculty who teach twenty-year-olds in general education courses. We are slowly seeing applications in which faculty are designing substantial, rigorous, and yet attractive courses or curricula for adults who may or may not have an interest in a degree.

One of the most ambitious of these projects is the Capital District Humanities Program of the State University of New York-Albany, which involved, in just over a year from mid 1979 to mid 1980, thirty-four separate programs, eighty-five humanities scholars from a number of regional colleges and universities, and an attendance of 15,000 persons.

The Future

Grant applications to NEH are retrospective; they reveal—even recent ones—work that was undertaken months or even a year or more ago. What about the coming decade? The critical issue is the faculty's readiness. There is no question of faculty ability, but only questions of faculty preparedness and will. Particularly, there cannot be much good happening in the next decade without a faculty prepared to take steps by which they acknowledge the whole of their institution as well as its parts. Dismissing the declining enrollments, changing income, cost of materials and energy, and so on as problems for the administration is a luxury of a bygone era.

With deliberate and detailed faculty planning, institutions can prosper only by generating FTEs through pandering to student interests and by making effective (if expedient) arguments to the state legislature that governs or funds them.

The Context for the Next Decade

Some generalizations can be made about our current circumstances and the potential of the next decade. From 1950 to 1970, new institutions of higher education were created in this country on an average of one a week: 1,886 to 2,573. In 1941 there were 1.5 million students in higher education; in 1975 there were 11 million (Finn, 1978, p. 22).

In the early years of the 1970s Congress debated higher education support and developed a principle that shows no signs of weakening; that is, Congress decided that it would support higher education by supporting students, not by supporting institutions. The blunt reality is this: Congress will not and probably cannot rescue institutions in this next decade: Some are going to close.

There seem to be three areas that might be explored in an effort to create the context that is necessary for the humanities to thrive in the next decade. These are areas of effort that are open to every faculty member in the humanities and do not require such things as the facilities of a major research university or an endowment based upon new oil-producing land. These areas are: programs for the public; programs of elementary and secondary schools; and reexamination of the relationship of the humanities curriculum to the world of commerce.

Public Programs

College and university faculty must begin to explore ways in which they can make their work—its nature, purpose, and value—fresh and real to the broad public. Specialization and growth affected the liberal arts after World War II so that professors no longer seem relevant to or perhaps even in touch with the concerns of most people.

Continuing education programs in the humanities are still in their infancy, and there are too few centers of effort to share the substance and methods of the humanities with adults who may or may not be seeking a degree. In an address to the Council of Graduate Schools in December 1980, Peter Drucker of the Claremont Graduate School said that in his judgment the future for graduate study may lie in the humanities; that is, in providing for technically trained adults insights into the questions that have always been the core of literature, history, and philosophy. There is much evidence, Drucker argued, that once individuals have mastered their appropriate vocational skills and after they have established a career, they commonly begin to look for more education in the areas that technical education has slighted. While there is evidence that adults learn best when the courses or materials have a focus, the typical academic organization of historical, literary, and philosophic materials and events does not provide a focus that is responsive to the broader, less professional adult interest in these subjects. New ways to present these materials and events must be found.

Most of the public is forced to contend with junk disguised as history, literary criticism, and philosophy because the genuine scholars in these fields are writing and speaking only to one another. One is struck with the irony that little seems to have changed in this respect in the last century. Jane Addams, the founder of Hull House in Chicago in 1889, reflected on her experience with this early experiment in adult education after Hull House had been in operation for twenty years. Her words are painfully relevant: "It seems sometimes as if the men of substantial scholarship were content to leave to the charlatan the teaching of those things that deeply concern the welfare of mankind, and that the mass of men get their intellectual food from the outcasts of scholarship, who provide millions of books, pictures, and shows, not to instruct and guide, but for the sake of their own final financial profit" (1961, p. 297).

Elementary and Secondary Education

Nearly everyone is aware of declining test scores and growing public dissatisfaction with the quality of pre-collegiate schooling. What is not as well known or appreciated by the public is the depth and width of the chasm that exists between the world of college and university professors and the world of precollegiate teachers. When colleges and universities decided that they were going to concentrate on the production of new college faculty and researchers, the schools were turned over to others. Creating a new and lively relationship between liberal arts colleges and the schools is going to be difficult, and the models that might be used are not obvious. Both groups have large and established bureaucracies; both groups have separate professional and administrative associations.

There are painful questions regarding the humanities in pre-collegiate and collegiate education. The public has, generally speaking, been given hours upon hours of instruction in literature, history, languages, and philosophy. Why then do so many Americans associate history exclusively with dates and kings and wars? Why do so many of us associate English with grammar? Why do so many of us associate philosophy with nothing substantial at all? The teachers of the liberal arts in this country have had a captive audience that would be the envy of any demagogue, and yet it seems we have not conveyed the delight, the excitement, the profundity, and the meaning of the fields that so engage us as teachers and as persons.

Liberal Arts and Commerce

Finally, we must establish a dialogue, without rhetoric, with the world of commerce. Every so often the chief executive officer of a major American corporation claims to value above all other things the education received in the liberal arts, and yet the recruiting staff that appears on campus issues a notice saying that it is prepared to meet all the accountants, computer programmers, and M.B.A.'s who can be rounded up. Humanities faculty frequently disparage the world of commerce as a hotbed of philistinism and various social evils.

Cooperative conversation between the liberal arts and commerce may make it possible to develop a curriculum, for example, that provides a base for a company to build upon and still consists of a major in the humanities. After all, most humanities graduates in this nation are working and only a minority are involved in teaching.

There seem to be several different approaches to the issue of the liberal arts and jobs that can be explored simultaneously. One is to reestablish within corporations an awareness that a liberal arts education does not incapacitate an individual. A broadly educated individual can be analytical, perceptive of larger issues related to particulars, responsive to people, articulate, able to write, and able to learn new fields—all qualities that companies seek, particularly in individuals who could become leaders.

Another approach is to modify the traditional humanities major program, undergraduate or graduate, so that the students are given some preparation for nonacademic careers. The program in internship and advisement developed by the sociology department at the University of Wisconsin, Whitewater, is an example, as is the Professional Skills Minor (or option) at Pennsylvania State University. In the latter, Ph.D. students in the liberal arts pursue a one-year program to develop research, analysis, and communication skills. The nature and use of computers and word processing play a role in this curriculum. In such programs as these, humanities and social science majors are able to give evidence that they have logically planned for a nonacademic career. These programs contrast with those that take place once a degree has been completed (such as a summer workshop) and thus appear as afterthoughts.

Still another option is the development of degree programs that have the humanities at their center but are designed for nonacademic careers. Perhaps the best known of such contemporary programs is public history. Public history programs train students in the methods and skills of the historian and couple those skills with internships in government, cultural institutions, and the corporate world. The University of California at Santa Barbara was the leader in developing the public history curriculum. Bowling Green State University is currently exploring the possibilities of what is being called "applied philosophy"; that is, a curriculum in philosophy modified by internship and other experience and designed for nonacademic careers. The list of examples of new humanities majors or programs is fairly extensive and include: a M.A. program in American Indian Policy Studies at the University of Arizona; a program in archival, museum, and editing studies at Duquesne University; and graduate courses for the practice of existential and phenomenological psychology at Seattle University.

The final matter to mention as part of establishing a dialogue between the liberal arts and commerce is career counseling for students. In the days when an undergraduate liberal arts student could choose among jobs, career counseling for students was relatively straightforward and mostly a matter of arranging interviews for the new graduates with firms and institutions. With increasing specialization, such counseling became a matter of matching specialized training with specialized recruiting. However, with a troubled economy, ever-increasing specialization, and an apparent surplus of those seeking employment, the liberal arts student became the odd person out. Many faculty members are unable to help with career advice, since they themselves have not encountered the same circumstances and have little experience upon which to draw.

Many institutions have recognized the need for new methods of student advising, and two can be mentioned. One is the sophisticated system of career counseling at the University of South Carolina, with its career-planning office for humanities and social science majors. The second is the effort by the Committee on Institutional Cooperation (a consortium of the Big Ten universities and the University of Chicago) to bring faculty and administrators together to discuss new possibilities in humanities education and counseling for humanities students.

Conclusion

Applications to NEH offer evidence for some optimism about the next decade, and the heart of that optimism is not so much that the ideas found in the applications are certain to triumph over the trials of declining resources, but because the applications are evidence that faculty are planning to help themselves and are not looking for a miraculous solution. There is a parallel lesson from Greco-Roman drama: The characters who waited for the *deux ex machina* found instead their nemesis—one suited uniquely to them.

References

Addams, J. *Twenty Years At Hull House*. New York: New American Library, 1961.

"Changing Numbers in High-School Graduating Classes." *Chronicle of Higher Education*, January 7, 1980, p. 8.

Commission on the Humanities. *The Humanities in American Life*. Berkeley: University of California Press, 1980.

Finn, C. E., Jr. *Scholars, Dollars, and Bureaucrats*. Washington, D.C.: The Brookings Institution, 1978.

National Center for Education Statistics. *Digest of Educational Statistics, 1980*. Washington, D.C.: National Center for Education Statistics, 1980.

Southern Regional Education Board. "The Search for General Education: The Pendulum Swings Back." In *Issues in Higher Education #15*. Atlanta: Southern Regional Education Board, 1979.

Geoffrey Marshall has taught as a professor of English at several universities and has had a long-standing interest in relating the humanities to the wider society. He is presently director of the Division of Education Programs at the National Endowment for the Humanities.

*A program developed by a sociology department is
offered as a model by which other liberal arts
disciplines can reassert those values and goals that
serve the intellectual and artistic development of
men and women. The program, involving the
combination of career with academic counseling,
internships, and other features, has been grafted on to
an existing, intellectually demanding curriculum.*

Careers, Curricula, and the Future of Liberal Learning: A Program for Action

Charles S. Green III
Hadley G. Klug
Lanny A. Neider
Richard G. Salem

Sociologists with Ph.D.'s, like people with Ph.D.'s in other liberal arts disciplines, have recently been forced to seek nonacademic employment (Cartter, 1976). The American Sociological Association (ASA) has become increasingly concerned (as have professional associations in other disciplines) with opening up nonacademic job opportunities (Panian and

The authors are in the Department of Sociology at the University of Wisconsin-Whitewater. The program described in this chapter was a wholly collaborative effort on the part of all members of the department, including, besides the authors, William L. Greer, Anton C. Mueller, Robert C. Sweet, and Mathew Zachariah. The department received the first annual Teaching Award of the Wisconsin Sociological Association for its development of this program. Portions of this chapter appeared in the February 1980 issue of *The American Sociologist* and are reprinted by permission of the American Sociological Association.

de Fleur, 1975; Foote, 1974). Unfortunately, the ASA and other professional associations have focused almost exclusively on expanding nonacademic opportunities for those with masters degrees and doctorates rather than for those with only undergraduate degrees. Yet undergraduates are far more numerous and are as troubled—if not more so—over the vocational uses of their degrees as are those with graduate degrees (Dayton, 1979; Terry, 1979).

We became especially concerned about undergraduates after reviewing the results of a survey completed in mid 1976 of our undergraduates who received their degrees in the years 1971–1975. We found that 27 percent of our graduates took their present job either as an interim one "until something better comes along" or because they had "nothing else from which to choose." Twenty-five percent reported "lots of trouble" finding work and an additional 33 percent reported they had had "some trouble" finding work. Over half our graduates thought our department or the university should have better prepared them for the job market.

A representative sample of comments to our open-ended question on how we could have better prepared students for the job market reveals just how severe their criticisms were:

- "More practical knowledge of the working world. Facts not fantasies!"
- "Remind you that your education, if for nothing else, is an experience for learning's sake and don't expect to find a job with it!"
- "Tell me that since I don't have much experience I'll have to settle for a lower-paying job to get experience. Offer an internship program."
- "I asked no help from anybody and got none. I have wasted five years and now I am going to begin looking for jobs in areas of interest to me."
- "Truthful answers regarding the real situation of the job market."
- "You people did nothing for me, no interest in me or my education."

One possible response to these sentiments would have been to modify both the content and variety of our courses, making them more practical (for example, Handcuffs 101) and thereby more immediately relevant. Many of our graduates urged us to do just that. Their position, apparently, would be supported by many sociologists concerned, as we were, with stable or declining enrollments (Green and others, 1980). We rejected such a position in informal discussions stretching over a period of several years; we reached a consensus that it was preferable for our department to die with dignity rather than compromise our intellectual integrity. But we also felt that we could not completely ignore our students' career concerns. As we sought to respond to those concerns in subsequent discussions, ideas emerged gradually, and we only later realized that they constituted a coherent program.

We have implemented what we believe is a viable alternative to diluting or vocationalizing the traditional curriculum. We retained a demanding curriculum for all majors, which includes within its thirty-three semester hours a required introductory course, two required courses in research methodology, a required course in theory, and a distribution requirement specifying that at least one course must be taken in four of five possible areas of concentration. But we grafted on to our curriculum a career-oriented program consisting of four interrelated parts.

The following discussion reviews this program. We will first consider the *Handbook for Sociology Students;* second, our "Career Path" counseling; next, our internship course; and, last, our Seminar in Career Development.

A Handbook for Sociology Students

The *Handbook for Sociology Students* is designed to provide all students with an integrated source of information on questions pertaining to curriculum, potential career opportunities (including graduate education), and faculty interests and activities. It begins with a short introduction designed to acquaint the student with the unique perspective that sociology has to offer. The second and largest section of the handbook suggests sources of career information and information on what may be required for further study at the graduate level. This section also points out a number of potential career areas, including business, personnel management, law enforcement, urban planning, social-services delivery, and government employment. In addition, this section includes a discussion of twenty-one career paths open to sociology majors. The discussion of each career path incorporates a suggested program consisting of sociology courses, courses for a minor, and electives.

Next, the handbook presents the major and minor degree requirements and provides descriptions of the department's course offerings and their content. Last, the handbook provides information on the faculty in our department. The professional biography for each faculty member conveys the diversity and depth of both academic and nonacademic experiences faculty can make available to students.

Career Path Counseling

We had experienced serious difficulties prior to the development of the current edition of the handbook, in trying to help students clarify their career objectives and develop an appropriate program of study. Although an earlier edition of the handbook had listed career options, it did not make plain to the student exactly what sorts of academic programs would be relevant to these options. Neither was it clear to our faculty how a program of study at the university might be constructed to prepare a student for any particular career. During a number of informal discussions there emerged the idea of developing the series of career paths alluded to earlier. A paper, "Career Paths in Sociology," was prepared by one of the authors and later included in the current edition of the handbook. This section not only informs students of the academic program required for each career path but also provides faculty with the information they need for combining career counseling with academic advising.

Most importantly, however, these career paths are more comprehensive than those areas of employment to which sociology majors have traditionally restricted themselves: social welfare, police, and corrections The twenty-one paths are grouped into three areas: (1) direct human services, (2) business corporations, and (3) administration and planning/ federal and state government. There are ten paths in the direct human services area, including "social welfare casework," "juvenile probation, residential and group home treatment," "vocational counseling," and "police." Next, there are six paths in the business corporations area, including "general management," "personnel management," and "general marketing." Lastly, there are five paths in the administration and planning/federal and state government area, including "management/ administration" and "research/planning analysis." Preparation for careers in specialized areas of business and administration/management (in the private as well as the public sector) have recently become viable options through the adoption by our College of Letters and Sciences of a "professional minor in business." This allows the sociology major to choose from a series of business emphases in preparation for employment in corporations or governmental agencies that seek individuals with broad liberal arts backgrounds but with some course work appropriate to their specialized needs. The descriptions of two widely divergent career paths are summarized below:

I. *Juvenile Probation, Residential and Group Home Treatment*
   A. Character of employment opportunities
      Local counties employ graduates with degrees in social welfare, sociology, or psychology as juvenile probation officers. There are also more positions available as counselors in both private, county, and state-operated group homes and treatment centers. The work of the juvenile probation officer centers on both treatment and control of juveniles referred by police (or schools) or declared "beyond parental control" by their parents. Specifically, the work of the probation officer involves examination of family and child problems, recommendations of disposition plans to the court, family counseling, acting as a referral agent to other agencies, and monitoring of the juveniles' behavior in the family, at school, and in treatment

settings. The group-home or treatment-center counselor, however, is most often concerned with the establishment of acceptable behavior patterns by youth at the group home or center. The counselor leads group counseling sessions, plans activities, deals with youth-family relations, and seeks to provide the establishment of an environment of trust and affection in which the young person can develop an acceptable level of self control.

B. Recommended Curriculum
  1. Sociology major to include:
      a. Introduction to Criminology
      b. Sociology of Minorities
      c. Juvenile Delinquency
      d. Applied Sociology
         (in this course the student is placed in an agency for practical experience)
  2. Psychology minor to include:
      a. Behavior Disorders
      b. Introduction to Clinical Psychology
      c. Interview and Psychotherapy Techniques
  3. If these courses not taken in psychology, then:
      a. Introduction to Social Welfare
      b. Social Welfare Methods I
      c. Social Welfare Methods II

II. *Management and Administration*
A. Character of employment opportunities
  There are substantial opportunities for graduates with B.A. degrees in sociology, political science, and public administration to obtain employment with the state of Wisconsin and the federal government (as well as in municipal government) in the area of management and administration. These opportunities exist in many areas, from personnel management through property management and contract administration. The state and federal agencies in which employment is available encompass a great range of specific activities, from criminal justice and corrections through agriculture, transportation, and consumer protection. Moreover, student internships (some of which are paid) and postgraduate traineeships (all of which are paid) are readily available.

B. Recommended Curriculum
  1. Sociology major to include:
      a. Sociology of the Future
      b. Bureaucracy and Democracy
      c. Applied Sociology
         (in this course the student is placed in a government agency most compatible with specific career goals)

2. Political science, public administration, and individualized general business or general management minor to include some of the following:
   a. Introduction to American Government and Politics
   b. Public Policy and Administration
   c. Data Processing (with Finite Mathematics for Business and Social Sciences as prerequisite)
   d. Management Concepts
   e. Accounting Concepts
   f. Public Finance (with Economic Principles, Problems and Policies I and II as prerequisites)

Career Path Counseling for Other Liberal Arts Disciplines

It can be argued that career path counseling is suitable only in those liberal arts disciplines such as sociology whose courses alone or in combination with more technically oriented courses provide an academic background immediately relevant to certain occupations. However, we contend (as does Arthurs, this volume) that virtually all the liberal arts disciplines develop those analytical and communications skills necessary for success in any professional career. Furthermore, we contend that when a major in any of these disciplines is supplemented with selected, technically oriented courses, this combination is *sufficient* preparation for the vast majority of entry-level professional and managerial positions. Why, then, do employers, students, and even academic administrators and faculty commonly see little career relevance in the undergraduate study of English literature, philosophy, or even chemistry?

The reason is that few faculty or administrators have challenged the assumption that students need to take a lengthy array of specialized technical and vocational courses to pursue careers. Our failure to challenge traditional curricula in business, education, engineering, and other vocational fields is in turn grounded in two circumstances: (1) challenge seems hopeless, given the lengthy time these curricula have been in place and the vested interests acquired in them; (2) once a discipline or program has been introduced into a college or university, it is subject to the academic courtesy that automatically accords equal legitimacy to every existing offering. Given our presumed expertise in and responsibility for curricular decisions, it is understandable that students have failed to mount a challenge. Moreover, it should be evident that employers fail to challenge traditional curricula because specialized technical and vocational courses amount to a massive and highly valuable subsidy for employers.

In addition, the array of business, education, or engineering courses typically forced on undergraduates appear intended to convince and reassure prospective employers that a quality product is being produced

(Kamens, 1977). To put it another way, lengthy arrays of narrowly specialized "how to do it" courses appear more demanding, even though the same substantive course content can be conveyed in one or two more general and more intellectually demanding courses. Appearances, in the form of transcripts, resumes, and other paper credentials, are the primary bases for employers' hiring decisions (Collins, 1979).

Given these present "realities," a B.A. degree with a major in philosophy *is* a profound impediment to the acquisition of an entry-level professional position. But is a person with such credentials necessarily incapable of performing well in an entry-level position? We think not. In a rapidly changing job market, genuine job security lies in having the flexibility for change and personal growth. Such flexibility is better provided by broad conceptual, analytic, and communication abilities than by specific skills or information. In furtherance of such flexibility, faculty must work with students in the development of academic programs that not only suit students' immediate needs to secure entry-level positions but also provide broad conceptual, analytic, and communication abilities. In order to develop these programs, it is essential that each liberal arts department design sample career paths for students, using selected courses from a number of areas. For example, could not a philosophy major be combined with a minor in computer science and selected business electives (Turnbull, 1980)? Or, could not an individual combine a philosophy major with a minor in finance, marketing, or even English with a technical-writing emphasis? The possible academic programs and associated career paths for a philosophy major are extensive. Not only are there opportunities in business and government for computer programmers and "systems analysts," but the minor (plus electives) can be used to prepare for openings in banking, securities management, editing, internal report writing, medical ethics consulting, and administrative or marketing research.

In summary, the issue is not whether career paths can be developed, but rather the willingness of liberal arts departments to take the responsibility for exploring the relevance of their discipline to employment in specific career areas. No less important is the willingness of faculty and administrators to realize the limitations and, indeed, the transient value of "professional" curricula in the development of abilities essential for both changing job markets and personal growth (Fowler, 1980; Gottcent, 1980).

Internship Program

Our internship placement program is an integral part of our effort to help students clarify career goals and gain specialized experiences appropriate to these goals. Applied Sociology (as our program is known) is designed as an elective for juniors and seniors who are majoring or minoring in sociology. Course credit (which is based on a formula according to hours worked) is given for approved placements in numerous agencies and organizations. The program was initiated during the summer session of 1976 and has had interns participating every semester since then. During this period a total of seventy-six placements have been made in the following areas: police and adult corrections (nineteen), juvenile corrections and group homes (sixteen), counseling/mental health/social services (twenty-nine), research/planning (five), administration/management (three), hospices/senior citizens centers (one), and personnel (three).

As might be expected, we have found that the most difficult aspects of an internship program are student indecision about the kind of placement they desire and the search for an organization or agency willing to take the time necessary to work with students. Luckily, many agencies see student interns as extra help at no expense (although on a number of occasions students have actually been paid). Students usually have at least a general idea about the kind of internship experience they would like (for example, "working with people" versus research/planning), but it is often necessary to suggest concrete alternatives as well as specify what sort of tasks and activities are expected. In most cases several alternatives are evaluated for each student through phone calls or visits by the coordinator. Approximately half of the placements are with agencies or departments that have not worked with our program before. Matching student to job is purely subjective. Since the coordinator has usually had some contact with the student through course work and at least a fairly lengthy interview, the coordinator takes into account such factors as verbal ability, personal assertiveness, and writing ability. Past grades are not taken into account and, most importantly, no student has been refused an internship. We see it as a right—not a privilege.

Probably the most time-consuming activity related to the program has been the effort to develop a network of contacts at agencies and organizations. The network has been painstakingly developed using techniques that range from simply calling an agency listed in the telephone directory and being referred from one person to the next until some results are achieved to contacting former students who now are employed. Contact with agencies is maintained through visiting supervisors for the purpose of evaluating student interns, lunching with past or current supervisors, or—on occasion—having agency people as guest speakers in class. Some placements are also used on a continuing basis. The program coordinator often combines student evaluation and lunch with one or more agency people, and, on occasion, even concludes an "evaluation" visit with a second, and more lengthy, visit to a local bar (along with the agency supervisor, of course).

In general, wide opportunities for career-related experience have been provided, ranging from such direct human services as police work and counseling (both individual and group) to evaluation research. Every agency has been willing to provide opportunities for students to become involved in a substantial range of activities at a particular agency. For example, one student who was placed with the city of Madison (Wisconsin) Police Department not only patrolled with police but also worked with the community relations, alcohol/drug abuse, detective, and youth-aid divisions. Moreover, shortly after her internship, she was one of sixteen new officers hired by the Madison Police Department from over 350 applicants.

Overall, supervisors have been cooperative in providing meaningful activities for students. There have been no placements where students have been ignored. In only one situation has agency personnel felt substantial dissatisfaction with the performance of a student. When the internship coordinator first learned of this problem (involving agency workers' perception of a "know it all" attitude on the part of the student), it was resolved quickly during a discussion with the student's supervisor.

No student has expressed dissatisfaction with the experiences gained at a particular placement. On the contrary, nearly all have been very positive. Nevertheless, whether placements have led invariably to specific careers (or at least to career clarification) is still not known. In most cases it will be necessary to evaluate the career consequences of internships the next time we survey our graduates. At this point our impression is that consequences vary widely. For example, one student's placement at the Rock County (Wisconsin) Office of Juvenile Probation led directly to his being hired as a full-time juvenile-probation officer. Yet another's placement at the same agency led to the change of her major from sociology to social welfare.

A Seminar in Career Development

The career seminar meets two hours per week for a semester and is offered as an elective to all sociology majors with junior or senior standing. Students receive credit for two semester hours; however, this credit is not applicable to major or minor requirements.

The objectives of the seminar include providing students with the information and skills necessary for selecting a graduate program, finding and obtaining jobs, managing career contingencies, and coping with ethical dilemmas at work. To achieve these objectives, traditional discussion methods and extensive, out-of-class reading assignments are supplemented by a series of exercises. These exercises are designed to force students to develop through actual experience the skills and knowledge of sources they need to find and obtain jobs without having to rely on the often poor services offered by employment agencies, college placement services, consultants, and so forth.

One such exercise, "The Quick Job Hunting Map," is assigned from Bolles' *What Color Is Your Parachute?* (1978). This exercise requires students to develop an inventory of their values, skills, and interests—an important prerequisite to finding satisfying and rewarding work. A second exercise, "Where Do You Want to Do It?," requires students to use the reference section of the library to find standard sources of information on: the future of employment, types of jobs, and salaries in various sectors of the economy; the names of and background information about executives; the products or services offered by various businesses, and government agencies; and climatological, demographic, social, economic, and political data on cities, states, and regions. Using these sources, students must find a minimum of three employers likely to have jobs of interest in each of three cities whose characteristics the students also find attractive. A third exercise, "Picking a Graduate Program," requires students to find and use standard sources of information in order to select three graduate programs that would provide the education or training relevant to the sorts of jobs in which they are interested. The fourth and fifth exercises, drawn from Figgins' *Techniques of Job Search* (1976), require students to write a resume and a letter of application and to correct examples of faulty letters provided in Figgins' book. "The Chutzpah Exercise" requires students to obtain personal information, preferably through an interview, about a national figure, such as Jane Fonda, or about a local notable, such as the mayor of Milwaukee. Suitable rewards are provided to those few who actually manage to obtain interviews—and much is learned by the discussion of the few successes and many failures.

Two rounds of videotaped, simulated interviews require students to put much of what they have already learned into practice. Each student is given a description of a real job from a newspaper or other source and urged to find out as much as possible about the job, the company or agency, and supervisor of that job. In further preparation, students must prepare an application letter and a resume specifically designed for that job. The first round of interviews is intended to expose each student to a fairly structured and low-stress interview situation. A student is first interviewed by another student playing the role of interviewer, that is, the supervisor or recruiter. When the interview is complete, the interviewer provides the interviewee with an evaluation on a check-off rating form. The students then switch roles. Later, students review their own video-tapes, evaluate them, and compare their evaluations with those provided by the interviewers. In the second round, students are assigned new partners. Interviewers are expected to conduct an unstructured and highly stressful interview. The seminar director reviews at least one video-tape from each student and provides additional constructive comments.

Each student's exercise write-ups are carefully critiqued and assigned a grade. However, students are permitted to revise and resubmit their work for a higher grade. This opportunity for revision encourages them to learn from their mistakes rather than feel only penalized for them.

Summary and Conclusions

In attempting to attract undergraduate majors and expand the job market for them, many have eloquently stressed the need for imaginative developments within the liberal arts curriculum. Others stress the impor- tance of pedagogical skill and technique in order to advance traditional liberal arts ideals within a new order of declining enrollments and con- stricting budgets. Yet the occupational opportunities considered suitable for liberal arts generalists depend to a very considerable extent upon the public's, and especially employers', understanding of and familiarity with the liberal arts. Few departments have sought to approach this problem of fulfilling the promise of the liberal arts by means of a program such as ours, which incorporates employment and employers into the learning process while maintaining the integrity of a traditional curriculum.

It is far too early to provide any definitive evaluation of our pro- gram. We do know that the reactions of our students to the internships, the handbook, the career seminar, and career path counseling have been highly favorable. Moreover, our class enrollments and our majors and minors have been increasing, whereas within our College of Letters and Sciences only three other departments or programs offering a major, all vocationally oriented (journalism, social welfare, and management computer systems), have experienced such increases; all other departments have experienced decreases. The College of Arts and the College of Education have expe- rienced decreases as well. Only within the College of Business and Econom- ics are there departments that have made substantial enrollment increases.

No one part of our program is unique. Other departments have developed handbooks for their majors (Vaughan, 1979). Internships and work-study programs such as Antioch's, Berea's, and Northeastern's are not innovative either (Task Force on Education and Employment, 1979). Other departments have recently developed "career paths" or "custom tracks" (Terry, 1979), though our tracks are more comprehensive than others', and we have gone further than most in combining academic counseling and career advising. We are perhaps unique in offering a career seminar through our department rather than through the university's placement service, but career seminars in general have a long history.

What, then, is unique about our program? We believe the program is unique in integrating all four parts into what is a traditional (albeit fairly rigorous) curriculum. More importantly, developing the program required us to rethink and clarify the purposes of the traditional undergraduate curriculum for liberal arts majors and, in so doing, to become aware of the necessity to include within its boundaries career planning and job-getting skills. We are convinced that we have found a viable answer to the perennial question: Do the liberal arts have a valid contribution to make as a prepara- tion for employment, as well as for graduate and professional schools and for later life? In addition, we think such a program fulfills the need to inform the public of what liberal learning is.

For example, we feel that the impact on employers of internships and the eventual full-time employment of more liberal arts graduates is such that employers will begin to evaluate more positively the usefulness of the liberal arts as career preparation. Indeed, our recently completed pilot survey of employers' criteria for employee selection suggests that such changes have already begun. Other survey data on employers reinforce this conclusion (Reiser and Maiolo, 1979). Moreover, we believe that liberal arts graduates in business and government can have a liberalizing impact on decision making within organizational structures and, thereby, on American society as a whole (Ebersole, 1979; Jacobs, 1974; Galbraith, 1967; Miner, 1971; Zald, 1978).

We feel that by sending out copies of our handbook to local schools and by speaking before school classes, we inform the public of what liberal learning is and convey the message to high school students, their parents, and their counselors that not only is liberal learning intrinsically important, but that you can indeed do something with a liberal arts degree.

Thus our program is designed as a partial solution to the crucial issue of the role colleges and universities should play in the larger society. One definition of that role has been provided by Clark Kerr who, in *The Uses of the University*, contends that: "The multiversity in America is perhaps best seen at work, adapting and growing, as it responded to the massive impact of federal programs beginning with World War II. A vast transformation has taken place without a revolution, for a time almost without notice being taken. The multiversity has demonstrated how adaptive it can be to new opportunities for creativity; how responsive to money; how eagerly it can play a new and useful role" (1963, pp. 38–39).

John Kenneth Galbraith apparently agrees with Kerr's definition by observing that: "Colleges and universities can serve the needs of the technostructure and reinforce the goals of the industrial system. They can train the people and cultivate the attitudes which insure technological advance, allow of effective planning and insure acquiescence in the management of consumer and public demand" (1967, p. 375).

But Galbraith refuses to accept Kerr's definition as the only one open to us. He, like Edgar Litt (this volume), believes the spirit of liberal education endures. Moreover, Galbraith believes that spirit can prevail because though "educators have yet to realize how deeply the industrial system is dependent on them," that very dependence gives us the power to choose and create a different role: "Colleges and universities can strongly assert the values and goals of educated men [and women]—those that serve not the production of goods and planning but . . . intellectual and artistic development" (1967, p. 376).

Clearly, we prefer Galbraith's choice. Although our program is designed to provide our graduates with some basic skills needed by employers, this objective is subordinated to that of providing our graduates with values and ideals that constitute the unique perspective of the liberal arts. We are therefore convinced that our program is worth emulating.

References

Bolles, R. N. *What Color Is Your Parachute?* Berkeley, Calif.: Ten Speed Press, 1978.

Cartter, A. M. *Ph.D.'s and the Academic Labor Market.* New York: McGraw-Hill, 1976.

Collins, R. *The Credential Society.* New York: Academic Press, 1979.

Dayton, P. "Point of View." *The Chronicle of Higher Education,* May 29, 1979, p. 80.

Ebersole, M. C. "Why the Liberal Arts Will Survive." *The Chronicle of Higher Education,* May 21, 1979, p. 48.

Figgins, R. *Techniques of Job Search.* San Francisco: Harper & Row, 1976.

Foote, N. N. "Putting Sociologists to Work." *The American Sociologist,* 1974, *9,* 124-134.

Fowler, E. M. "Engineers: The Future Challenge." *The New York Times,* June 25, 1980, p. 13.

Galbraith, J. K. *The New Industrial State.* Boston: Houghton Mifflin, 1967.

Gottcent, J. H. "Practicing the Science of Getting Good Grades." *The Chronicle of Higher Education,* December 8, 1980, p. 58.

Green, C. S., Klug, H., Neider, L., and Salem, R. "Coping with Vocationalism: Careerism Versus Humanism in the Undergraduate Curriculum." Paper presented at annual meetings of the American Sociological Association, 1980.

Jacobs, D. "Dependency and Vulnerability: An Exchange Approach to the Control of Organizations." *Administrative Science Quarterly,* 1974, *19* (1), 45-59.

Kamens, D. "Legitimating Myths of Educational Organization." *American Sociological Review,* 1977, *42* (2), 208-219.

Kerr, C. *The Uses of the University.* Cambridge: Harvard University Press, 1963.

Miner, J. B. "Changes in Student Attitudes Toward Bureaucratic Role Prescriptions During the 1960s." *Administrative Science Quarterly,* 1971, *16,* 351-364.

Panian, S., and de Fleur, M. L. *Sociologists in Non-Academic Employment.* Washington, D.C.: The American Sociological Association, 1975.

Reiser, C., and Maiolo, J. "Sociologists in Private Enterprise: The Job Market for Non-Ph.D. Sociologists." *The Southern Sociologist,* 1979, *10,* 16-18.

Task Force on Education and Employment, National Academy of Education. *Education for Employment. Knowledge for Action.* Washington, D.C.: Acropolis Books, 1979.

Terry, G. B. "Our Professional Responsibilities Toward Job Skills and Job Shopping for Our B.S. and B.A. Graduates." *The Southern Sociologist,* 1979, *10,* 3-6.

Turnbull, A. D. "Wanted: Humanists to Write Computer Manuals." *The Chronicle of Higher Education,* October 20, 1980, p. 36.

Vaughan, C. A. "Career Information for Sociology Undergraduates." *Teaching Sociology,* 1979, *7* (1), 55-64.

Zald, M. N. "On the Social Control of Industries." *Social Forces,* 1978, *57,* 79-102.

Charles S. Green III is professor of sociology at the University of Wisconsin-Whitewater.

Hadley G. Klug is assistant professor at University of Wisconsin-Whitewater.

Lanny A. Neider is professor and chair, Department of Sociology at the University of Wisconsin-Whitewater.

Richard G. Salem is associate professor of sociology at the University of Wisconsin-Whitewater.

A public liberal arts college has devised a multi-faceted, occupational-development program to demonstrate the value of liberal learning to both students and potential employers.

A Liberal Education and Occupational Development

James W. Parins

The pressure for occupational-skills development for college students has grown during the 1970s and made profound changes on many campuses. While these changes are evident almost everywhere, the most drastic alterations in curriculum, staffing, and even institutional direction have taken place at the urban colleges and universities, schools with large concentrations of part-time, commuter, career-oriented students.

The very nature of the student population at these institutions has determined the occupational-skills emphasis that many of the urban schools have taken. For many of these students, their college experience takes on only secondary or tertiary importance, coming after the more pressing demands of job and family. College is seen as a training program that results in a more satisfying and more lucrative occupational position for the student, which in turn is expected to enhance the family life-style. This education is tied closely to career expectations and is seldom looked upon as training for life, a concept abandoned to students of more traditional "Ivy-league" colleges or attributed to times long past. For today's urban university student, education is pragmatic and its effect is immediate. The student sees the time and effort spent at school worthwhile only if the investment pays off next month or next year, and only if the rewards are tangible ones.

Given this situation, the urban university is faced with some issues that drastically affect curriculum and personnel planning, the school's competitive position for students, formula funding and most other means of support, and, most importantly, the nature of the institution. While these career-education issues are important to other institutions as well, they are no more acute than at those schools serving metropolitan areas. Since the urban colleges have had to deal for a long time with a high level of pressure for occupational-skills development, it may be helpful to study their responses to what is often perceived as a jarring confrontation between traditional values and timely change. The purpose here is to examine one such response, that of the College of Liberal Arts of the University of Arkansas-Little Rock (UALR).

UALR has long seen its educational role as being different from those of its sister institutions in the state, describing itself as having an "urban mission." At first glance, this may seem inappropriate for a university located smack dab in the middle of an agricultural state. The description is accurate, however, in view of the region that the school serves; the Little Rock and central Arkansas area is the population, governmental, and business-financial center of the state. Because of its unique position, it is natural for UALR to offer its services to this constituency, calling this effort its urban mission.

Throughout its history, the institution has seen career education as an important although not dominant part of its curriculum. The university began as Little Rock Junior College in 1927, when it was housed in buildings provided by the Little Rock public school district. Later, in 1957, it became a private, four-year educational institution, Little Rock University. During this period, the school offered a standard arts and science curriculum to its students, almost all of whom were natives of central Arkansas. While the liberal arts and traditional sciences provided the basis for the curriculum, many students were attracted to the schools of education and business, both of which offered direct employment opportunities.

The urban mission, with its emphasis on career education, came to be articulated as a basis for campus policy and direction only in the early 1970s, however, shortly after the merger of Little Rock University and the University of Arkansas system. The establishment of the University of Arkansas system dictated that each campus undergo a rigorous self-examination and that a mission statement be formulated as a result of this process. For UALR, this meant that its historical commitment to the local citizens, the demands of an urban student population, and its own need to establish a mission unique in the state system came together to greatly influence policy in terms of institutional direction.

Initial reaction to the articulation of the urban mission was mixed. Many faculty members and departments believed the new policy, with its emphasis on community involvement, applied research, and career development, provided new opportunities for the institution, its students, and its faculty. Others, however, regarded the trend as an ominous one, leading inexorably to the collapse of humanistic values and traditional educational standards. For the most part, the response by individuals and academic units was along lines that one might expect. English literature specialists, historians, and philosophers voiced fears about institutional abandonment of the liberal arts curriculum, while journalism, marketing, and engineering professors hailed the new age. While persons in some disciplines saw career education as a proper response to the needs of the community, others, most notably those in the liberal arts, saw it as a totalitarian concept. The practice of using the university to tailor individuals so that they fit the needs of the business and governmental powers was seen as inappropriate and even immoral.

Despite the division of opinion, it soon became clear that the trend would continue. In a few years, enrollment at UALR rapidly increased from around three thousand to ten thousand. Much of the growth was attributed to the attraction of new programs, many with clear occupational objectives. New departments—radio, TV, and film, for example—were created by the central administration to fill a perceived community need. For many in the traditional disciplines, the message was abundantly clear: areas that had not concerned themselves with career education in the past—especially elements of the liberal arts—would need to do so. Failure in this regard would mean a withering of traditional programs and a resulting inability for many to continue to practice their professions, the teaching of humanities or social sciences. Many reasoned that such a course would leave professors out of work, students uneducated in subjects deemed essential to their happiness, society poorer, and the republic weakened. Thus, various members of the faculty sought to fashion a program that would take them out of the dilemma.

The College of Liberal Arts sought to respond to the problem in a positive way. The idea was to demonstrate the value of a liberal arts education as an asset to the career seeker. The message, of course, had to be carried not only to the student as a potential job applicant but also to business and governmental leaders as potential employers. Both groups needed to be convinced that skills such as the ability to express oneself articulately by the spoken and written word are important in the "real" world. They needed to recognize that analytical skills fostered by the traditional liberal arts disciplines could be put to practical use outside the classroom. It was decided that these ideas could best be demonstrated by a multi-faceted approach. The College of Liberal Arts put into effect a program involving a citizens' advisory council, internship programs for students, vigorous placement activities for liberal arts graduates, a newsletter, and curriculum development.

The citizens' advisory council was put into effect in an attempt to bring the college and the community closer together. The idea was to set up a two-way channel of communication between the faculty and leaders in government and business. While the channel first operated only one-way—with ideas coming into the college—the community leaders soon became aware of potential areas of cooperation involving both students and faculty. One result was an increase in the use of faculty as consultants. Professors in political science and sociology, for example, conduct opinion surveys for political and business organizations. History professors work in various cultural heritage and restoration projects in the area. English professors offer composition and grant-writing workshops to governmental agencies, teach creative writing in nursing homes and the public schools, and have rewritten the state income tax instructions. Contacts made by the council have been obviously good for consultancy activity. The council has also brought the college and community closer together. It furnishes advice to the college from the outside and provides input from the college into certain business and governmental affairs. The council is a new project, and we look for more mutual benefits as the idea grows and matures.

While the council is in just its embryonic state, the student internship program has been functioning for a number of years. The program's organization is fairly standard and routine. Each department in the college has an intern coordinator who makes contact with area organizations and agencies, makes arrangements between the student and the student's employer, and oversees the credit-granting aspects of the program. Students demonstrate to the coordinator's satisfaction their willingness and ability to participate. When the intern sponsor indicates a willingness to use an intern with particular skills, the coordinator attempts a match-up by sending the student for an interview. If the interview is successful, a contract is signed by all parties. Contract provisions typically include the employer's pledge to pay the minimum wage and to provide on-the-job training and an agreement between coordinator and student concerning written assignments. The program has served to furnish more than 100 students per semester with valuable training. It also aids in the recruitment of liberal arts graduates into government and business; this is a direct way of demonstrating the communication and analytical skills of students trained in the traditional disciplines. Another benefit is that the students and the college make contacts in the community. More important, though, are those lasting relationships formed because of the program's existence. One of the greatest intangible benefits is that the image of the college as a vital community resource is enhanced.

Another part of the program is the placement activity for liberal arts graduates. The associate dean of the college has established close ties with the university placement bureau. The associate dean coordinates the activities of the bureau with those of the college, making sure, for example, that liberal arts students are aware of appropriate openings or are setting up interviews with recruiters. The student makes contact with the members of the advisory council and makes follow-ups after internships are completed. The associate dean also arranges to have the biographies of graduates carried in the college newsletter.

In addition to printing the graduates' biographies, the newsletter seeks to publicize the college philosophy. The newsletter is sent to community leaders as well as to recruitment officials in various business and governmental organizations. Written by students who are writing interns, it serves as a demonstration of their skills while it spreads the word on the efforts of interns in other areas. Each issue features the students and faculty of one of the departments in the college and examines the programs in which they are involved. The newsletter is important for publicity of a general nature, and it also serves to aid placement and particular programs.

Curriculum development is another area that concerns the college, but, especially as it relates to career decisions, the curriculum must be tied to effective advisement. An examination of the advisement system showed that there was good initial contact with the students, but little in the way of formal advising thereafter, except a degree-plan session when a major is selected. As a result, there was little opportunity to suggest ways to students to enhance their marketability at graduation time. The advisement system is at present being redesigned by the associate dean. The goal is to provide on-going advisement that would alert students to the idea of marketing their skills from early on. At the same time, students would be urged to select degree plans with career-oriented courses and programs from inside and outside liberal arts. Expository and technical writing, information and communication systems, and computer skills are examples of areas of instruction that are being suggested.

New programs that exploit traditional liberal arts are also being developed. The Department of Psychology recently began offering a M.A. in Applied Psychology. The education and skills provided by this degree program are in great demand by central Arkansas businesses and government agencies. Graduates go directly into work as industrial psychologists and personnel managers. For several years, the English and journalism departments have offered a joint baccalaureate degree in Professional and Technical Writing. In addition, the English department offers a writing minor. Response to these two programs has been overwhelming, placing heavy demands on the staff. The enrollment in the writing courses has more than offset the dwindling numbers in the literature courses. Another program that promises to attract students while increasing their marketability is a new B.A. combining economics, other business courses, and liberal arts courses. It is intended as a well-rounded program for students who seek careers in business, government, and the law.

While many of these changes are new, the college is already beginning to feel the effects. One effect is increased enrollments, a trend that is not shared by liberal arts programs across the nation. In 1980, for example, while the overall university went up 3 percent, the College of Liberal Arts showed an increase of just over 6 percent. But enrollment alone is no measure of success; the key, of course, is placement. While the data are not yet sufficient to make a positive judgment on the program's effectiveness in this regard, the signs are very encouraging. We have received significant, positive reactions from the intern program, and we have some intangible signs that indicate we are moving in the right direction. For example, a comparison of recent interview schedules from placement bureaus with those of a year or two ago shows that companies are much more willing to consider liberal arts graduates now than they were then.

The impact on the community has been important. We have sensed an increase in interest in the college and in the liberal arts generally. A conference on the future of the humanities sponsored by the college and held on our campus in spring of 1980 was well attended by members of the business community. We have seen an increase in consultancies for faculty members as well, a sign that liberal arts skills are valued in the society. In this willingness to make use of the college's faculty, students, alumni, and other resources, we have discovered two things on the part of the community: a new sense of what the college is all about and a sense of common purpose.

The impact on the college has been profound as well. Good students are now recruited into liberal arts programs more easily because they have more confidence in the education and skills they receive. And there are intangible rewards for the liberal arts faculty as well for having undertaken such a program. Two of the most important are a sense of purpose and a sense of achievement. For many unlucky professionals, these are never experienced.

James W. Parins is professor of English and assistant dean for public service in the College of Liberal Arts at the University of Arkansas at Little Rock. He has published several works, including a number of computerized studies of literary works, a textbook, a critical book on the Victorian poet William Barnes, and a bibliographic guide to American Indian writers.

*To the extent that liberal education is a servant of self
and society, it will be very careful about what
students think they want and for what society expects
and will pay for. To the extent that liberal education
is a critic of self and society, it will concentrate on
providing the tools, the discipline, the attitudes, and
the historical perspectives for critical examination
of self and society.*

Career and Curriculum: A Philosophical Critique

Ronald Jager

During the 1970s, enrollments in college courses shifted away rather drastically from the liberal arts, especially the humanities, toward courses in disciplines with a specifically professional orientation. That is the well known fact, perhaps the most distressful one, about the college scene. It is widely expected by those whose talent it is to expect things on our behalf that the trend will continue through the 1980s, or at least through the foreseeable future. Something variously called "vocationalism," or "careerism," or sometimes even "professionalism" has been let loose in the colleges and is sweeping nearly everything in its path. Since it cannot very well be stopped—or anyhow will not be, say some—we shall have to find a way to live with it. Indeed, it can seem as if there is hardly an educational topic on the college agenda but that it turns out to be some near or remote variation on the present pace of galloping vocationalism and the methods of reining it or indulging it.

Shall we spatter the liberal arts curriculum with practical and applied courses? Shall we soften the intellectual core, make the stuff easier and simpler to match the practical bent of the restless student? Shall we, that is, take the old curriculum in hand and either spice it up or dilute it? No, No, none of these, say some authors in this volume.* "There is a viable alternative to tinkering with the curriculum." They would have us admit that the liberal arts are in an ivory tower, and they are willing to try to get the students off the streets and into the tower for a time—provided we can show them the way back.

They imply something like this: It is not just that part of the liberal arts are useful (the jazzed-up or watered-down parts), nor that they are useful if altered; no, the whole shebang is good and useful pretty much as it is, or was. But it takes a bit of hard looking and planning to demonstrate that: The kids have to be shown. Hence the supplemental program to help students see, for example, how liberal learning naturally finds its way back to reality, how the traditional curriculum left intact and furnished with more sensitive road maps is still the best curriculum. The four-part program (for sociology students, in this particular case) includes a handbook, careful career-path delineation and counseling, an aggressive internship program, and a term-long optional seminar in career development. Nothing all that spectacular, say the designers, quite rightly—realizing that at the very least it is a well-developed system of academic coaching.

In a sense it is hard to do anything but applaud the plan. Few of us have intellectual tastes so austere and fastidious as to despise such wholesome efforts to help students get their bearings. Indeed, on the face of it there seems to be no good reason at all why other departments, other colleges, could not do something along similar lines. But support for this particular program, however, does not prevent one from commenting on the sort of ideas and circumstances that prompt strategies like it.

The content and value of the liberal arts—that is one issue; how to get students to understand, act on, and profit from the liberal arts studies— that is a different issue. The first is, broadly, a question of substance; the second is a question of technique. It can be misleading to let these run together, as the authors are sometimes tempted to do. Thus, one should not necessarily sum up their program quite in their way: they look at it as a "viable answer to that perennial question: Do the liberal arts have a valid contribution to make as preparation for employment, as well as for graduate and professional schools, and for later life?" The answer to *that* question is this: Valid contribution? Yes of course—though saying so is essentially a testimony of the faith that keeps us engaged in this enterprise of liberal education. It is not the substantive "contribution" of the humanities that is in question or to which they provide an answer. The question they answer is a very practical one, and they answer it not by dealing

---

*The point of departure and the recurrent example in this chapter is the program in sociology at the University of Wisconsin-Whitewater as described by Professors Green, Klug, Neider, and Salem in their chapter in this volume. Comments are also applicable to the Marshall and Parins chapters in this volume.

directly with the humanities or the liberal arts, but by dealing wisely and pedagogically with students' career concerns.

In the Editors' Notes to this volume they write:"The career concerns of our undergraduate students are real, compelling, and legitimate." Well, they are real and compelling all right. Their legitimacy is a somewhat more complicated question, and we should look at some of the elements in the lineage of that concern. What is it we need to think about in order to consider the legitimacy of the students' concerns? Three things come to mind.

For one thing, our culture has developed the means (often willy-nilly) and encouraged the attitudes (often inadvertently) to ensure that students entering college will feel uneasy if they lack swift, clear answers to questions of this kind: What are you going to do with your education? What are you studying for? It will not really do, the student senses, to say: "For now, I'm studying mainly literature and sociology." Something so confident and flat-footed sounds evasive. What is the effort *for?* It is understood that "to get a good education and then on that basis decide what to do" is an unacceptable answer. Never mind that the teenager may not yet have encountered more than one inspiring teacher or may have talent for a subject not yet heard of—philosophy or hydrology, say—the teenager is already supposed to have a pretty definite idea about what this college education is to be good for. True, it is permissible to change your mind, but do it twice and somebody is sure to notice; the eventual letter of recommendation may read in part "after a considerable period of vacillation he has now decided upon his major."

The pressure of this vague burden of professionalism upon the beginning college student is most regrettable: unfair to students as individuals, subversive to educational values, and thoroughly unfortunate as social policy. If so, we probably ought to do more than we now do to shore up the frail and precious confidence some students feel in their education as the primary thing for now, and the use to which they will put it as a secondary thing. But whatever their attitudes, we shall not often change them with a speech or an essay or a law, so there is all the more reason for trying to understand them. Whether legitimate or not, the student's career concern is to some degree the predictable by-product of public expectations.

For another thing, a great deal can be said—little of it flattering—about the economic or material ambitions of the students of the "me-generation," and about the pragmatism and sense of immediacy that seems so natural to them. This need not be elaborated here. But facts of that sort, having to do with *private values,* even when supplemented by the impressive facts of *public expectations* mentioned above, do not yet adequately account for the shifting patterns of enrollment and attitude that concern us.

Accordingly, having mentioned these two kinds of facts, a third sort can be considered.

One important, underlying fact is often ignored in the familiar reviews of reasons for the careerist mentality. The academy and the curriculum are feeling the effects of a larger cultural phenomenon, and shifting academic interests are a striking symptom of it. A clumsy but accurate name for that phenomenon is the "professionalization" of modern life; it seems far more inexorable than either those private values or public expectations that are often so dismaying. Student attitudes did nothing to bring about the professionalization of life. But they do fall in line with it, and they do dramatize it.

Every aspect of our public life is now marked with the tracks of professionals of one sort or another: experts, consultants, specialists, resource persons, researchers, advisors, counselors, and coordinators, to say nothing of planners, designers, directors, programmers, facilitators, evaluators, and auditors. Nowadays not very much gets done without several of these types. We are witnessing an unprecedented extension of the role of professional work, its penetration of every nook and cranny of life. Even an innocent sociology student in a state university in Wisconsin is confronted with at least twenty-one different kinds of professions to join!

The expansion of professionalism (both as statistical fact and, more importantly, perhaps, as psychological attitude) is easy to relate to prominent social facts. Such facts range all the way from the general contours of the national agenda (husbanding diminishing resources, managing forms of scarcity, and institutionalizing various forms of retrenchments, which nobody desires) to very personal efforts to observe the regulations, prevent lawsuits, master the bureaucracy, and find the local margins of free choice. Quite understandably, the project of modern living elicits appeals to counsel, advice, and authority. We amateurs need the help of professionals if only to cope with the professionals that seem to be arrayed all about us.

The patterns seem everywhere the same. If the teachers get a lawyer, the school board will get one too. Rampant professionalism inspires in us not confidence but deference. The chairperson who once simply cast an eye over the scene and made a decision now appoints a task force, and the task force hires a consultant, a consultant who can tell them what the experts are thinking. Where once the committee looked into the problem and brought a report to the voters, now the committee has a budget and engages a licensed engineer who confers with the authorities and with a certified surveyor; the transactions are recorded by a trained stenographer and in accordance with the law; the computer time is allotted and plotted, and the books are checked by an official auditor.

The significant fact here is not red tape, regulations, or the bureaucracy. Those favorite scapegoats, when not largely fantasized, are frequently only the symptoms of the underlying professionalization of life that itself grows apace, even while the red tape is being cut and the regulations changed. Every day we make it harder to accomplish something without the complicity of expertise. If there are twenty-one kinds of former sociology majors to minister to our needs, and a like number for every other discipline of the liberal arts, to say nothing of the traditional professions, there must be a lot that we cannot handle. It would require full-time devotion of energy to retain the innocence of amateurism.

This is not an evaluation of this general circumstance—regrettable through it may be—but an identification of an underlying fact whose message seeps into the consciousness of today's youth. It is from such an awareness that a student contemplates the idea of a college education. To such a student it appears that this is no world for amateurs (they turn out to be the laborers); if there is to be more learning, from here on it has to be learning to cope. The message, vague and insistent, thus includes the idea that beyond the horizon of college is a world essentially composed of various sorts of professionals—specialists in something, people with an angle giving them an edge; and they are dealing with certain social "problems" or public "programs," or at least with the advancement of private careers within such a world. This is not a notably inspiring image of things.

But if that *is* the basic framework of social reality as mediated to our college-oriented teenagers—at just that time in life when they may finally be getting outside themselves to see their connections with a larger world— it is no wonder that the liberal arts have the aspect of an awkward hangover from another and slightly obsolescent order of reality. Well, yes, if we insist, they will oblige us with a modest inspection tour through a safe corner of that odd terrain; but since they are solemnly on their way somewhere else, is it not a bit of an irrelevancy? Then, a bit flustered by the dissonance, we find ourselves urging that "some of this is good for you" and feel that the homily registers on the students and reverberates on the overly professionalized society at large as the weakest form of special pleading. And it is. We had wanted to talk deeply about the purposes and values of liberal learning in a democratic society and about individual self-development through appropriation of the cultural heritage, and we somehow got diverted into shallowly applying Shakespeare to the newspaper and something from the Greeks to Richard Nixon. Lacking any context of humane learning and mutual awareness, we made an insipid case.

One of the implications of these remarks is that our beginning college students may seem to us (may seem even to themselves) less inspired than compelled: compelled by concerns of self, pressures of society, and the overarching professionalization of life. How very important it is, then, that the college and its implied idea of learning hold out for the student an alternate, more inspiring, and enobling image of human affairs. The question is whether that can be done successfully where our theory of education is muddled.

To oversimplify a bit: One can think of liberal education as essentially a *servant* of self and society, or as essentially a *critic* of them. To the extent that it is servant, it will be very careful about what students think they want and for what society seems to expect and will pay for; to the extent that it is critic, it will concentrate forthwith upon providing the tools, the discipline, the attitudes, and the historical perspectives for critical examination of self and society within the whole context of western civilization. Where the critic is the guiding image, the informing standpoint is simply the cultural heritage, which is also the substance of the curriculum. Where the servant is the guiding image, the standpoint is the self and the self's society. Of course, this is a matter of degree and emphasis, and in practice we shall likely be involved in both. But unless we have a definite *prior* notion as to what we are *principally* doing, we lack a firm reference point for thousands of individual actions all down the line. If education is primarily to serve student and societal interests just as these appear, whole patterns of curricular emphasis will follow rather naturally.

Liberal learning understood as servant in the sense implied above seems still to be a modern heresy, not less heretical because so pervasive, so tempting, so nearly inescapable. It would be in accord with this faith that one would, for many reasons, prefer to see students fall in love with, say, sociology as a branch of study and of research and practice, decide to major in it for its intellectual appeal, and then cast about for ways to make a living doing what they love, and know is important for them. But that ordering of priorities takes formidable courage, courage colleges could be doing more to support.

The professionalization of life imposes whole patterns of demands upon the college curriculum; it constantly inclines us to see that curriculum in utilitarian terms rather than in terms of our cultural heritage; and it subverts imagination by encouraging conformity to *what is*. Accordingly, one basic question it raises everywhere for the liberal arts in the context of the subjects discussed in this volume is this: Are students being given the kind of education that will make them observant and thoughtful critics of the very professionalization of life they are adapting to? Or does the education we offer instill a compliance more skillful than critical?

The program in sociology described by Wisconsin professors is really on the side of what I am calling the critic's view of education. Certainly their words at the end of their chapter testify to that idea. It is not wholly clear to what extent this view of education, which we share, is for them a solemn afterthought rather than an initial guiding thought. One can easily be pessimistic about the general ability of the liberal arts curriculum to retain for the coming decades anything like its traditional function and rationale unless it constantly reaffirms that function and that rationale, in the full awareness that its mission goes increasingly against the grain of student and societal presumptions.

However, defending the liberal art is not exactly a cheerless enterprise, precisely because it is an eloquent part of this defense that education frequently prompts people to see the light and impels them to change their minds, their values, or their whole way of looking at things. For some at least, the liberal arts, once thought a detour or a frill, are ultimately appropriated as central and basic. The hardest trick is to get people to sit more or less still for four years and get thoroughly immersed in all the evidence.

Ronald Jager is currently humanist-in-residence for the New Hampshire State Legislature. He was formerly associate professor of Philosophy at Yale University and has served as a curriculum consultant to a number of small liberal arts colleges. His major recent publications deal with the work of Bertrand Russell.

*The editors of this volume review the ideas presented
and offer further resources.*

Summary and Resources for Change

Charles S. Green III
Richard G. Salem

Summary

In our "Editors' Notes" we noted the massive shift of enrollments
that occurred in the 1970s from the liberal arts to vocational fields. The
chapters in this volume discussed two issues created by this enrollment
shift: why the shift has taken place and what the response of the liberal arts
should be.

We have seen from Solmon's and Litt's chapters that employers'
selection criteria and students' choice of majors, combined with government regulatory and budgetary decisions, have resulted in the massive
pressures to vocationalize course content and curricula that colleges and
universities are now experiencing. The next four chapters have a common
theme: that the liberal arts must resist the pressure to vocationalize by
reasserting the importance of those values intrinsic in traditional liberal
learning. The following three chapters argue that while the preservation of
the values of traditional liberal learning is absolutely necessary, it is not a
sufficient response. Implicit in these chapters is a redefinition of the role of
college and university faculty: those who take seriously their responsibili-

ties for undergraduate education must broaden their teaching to include both new audiences and the provision of both career and academic advising. The programs developed at Whitewater and Little Rock, for example, are designed to convince various segments of the public (public and private employers, high school and college students, parents, and counselors) that liberal learning is intrinsically valuable and that, indeed, you can do something with a liberal arts degree. What these chapters neglect are the difficulties that must be overcome in introducing such programs.

Introducing a new program into a single department can be accomplished relatively easily—*if* there is no opposition and *if* the innovator is willing to take sole responsibility for supervising interns, visiting high schools, writing handbooks, and advising students! Effecting change on a wider scale can be even more difficult. But as Marshall noted in this volume, innovation will be imperative if liberal learning is to survive, let alone thrive, in the decades ahead. The resources for change listed below are offered for the use of the innovators among our readers.

Resources for Change

Career Information Resources for Undergraduates:
1. *Department Career Resource Centers.* In a room housing such a center there might be (1) graduate catalogs; (2) information on financial aid for graduate students; (3) general publications on careers in your disciplines; (4) newsletters and employment bulletins from your discipline; (5) readable journals in your discipline (for example *Science 81, Society*); (6) selected materials on interviewing for jobs, determining career goals, and resume writing (see below for further details). Such a center can be established and maintained by students themselves. Center activities might include invitations to alumni to speak on their careers, a newsletter for alumni, and applied research.

For more specific ideas on establishing such a center, write Howard L. Sacks, Department of Anthropology/Sociology, Kenyon College, Gambier, Ohio 43022.

Resource materials on interviewing, determining career goals, and so forth, for a center might include:

Bolles, R. N. *What Color is Your Parachute?* (rev. ed.), 1980.
College Placement Annual.
Federal Career Directory. United States Civil Service Commission.
Figler, H. D. *PATH—A Career Workbook for Liberal Arts Students*, 1975.
Graduate Study in Management. Admission Council for Graduate Study in Management.
Lathrop, R. *Who's Hiring Who.* 1976.
Malnig, L. R., and Pell, A. R. *What Can I Do With a Major in . . .?* 1975.
Place, I., and Armstrong, A. *Management Careers for Women.* 1975.

Powell, C. R. *Career Planning and Placement for the College Graduate of the 70's.* 1974.

Pre-Law Handbook. Association of American Law Schools, The Law School Admission Council, and Educational Testing Service, 1976.

Strickland, R. *How To Get Into Law School.* 1974.

Walker, J. H., III. *Thinking About Graduate School.* 1973.

2. *Handbooks and Information Packets.* An alternative or supplement to a resource center is a handbook or information packet available to prospective majors through your college or university admissions office and through your own department.

For an example of a handbook, write either of the editors of this volume: Department of Sociology, University of Wisconsin-Whitewater, Whitewater, WI 53190.

For an example of an information packet, write Professor Charlotte A. Vaughan, Department of Sociology, Cornell College, Mt. Vernon, Iowa 52314.

3. *Career Seminars.* A detailed syllabus and copies of the exercises used in the seminar described in the chapter by Green, Klug, Neider, and Salem in this volume may be obtained by writing Green at the Department of Sociology, University of Wisconsin-Whitewater, Whitewater, WI 53190.

Combining Career with Academic Advising:

For excellent examples of career combined with academic advising, see: Emil T. Hofman and Peter P. Grande, "Academic Advising: Matching Students' Career Skills and Interest"; Ed Watkins "Integrating the Life Development Concept into the Curriculum." Both articles appear in Watkins, E. (Ed.). *New Directions for Education, Work, and Careers: Preparing Liberal Arts Students for Careers,* no. 6. San Francisco: Jossey-Bass, 1979.

An important prerequisite to combining career with academic advising is the development of career paths of the sort discussed in this volume by Green, Klug, Neider, and Salem. The first step in career-path development is acquiring a knowledge of what sorts of jobs are already held by people with undergraduate degrees in your discipline *and* what sorts of *additional* jobs they might be qualified to hold.

The latter information can be acquired with surveys of employers— a time-consuming and costly effort for a single department to undertake on its own. A more economical, albeit less satisfactory, approach is the careful examination of the job descriptions contained in the United States Department of Labor's *Dictionary of Occupational Titles,* a basic reference available in most college or university libraries.

Knowledge of the sorts of jobs already held by people with undergraduate degrees in your discipline can be obtained in one or more of the following ways: (a) from the placement office records of your own college or university; (b) from your own surveys of alumni; (c) alumni surveys or placement office data available from other colleges and universities. Sources for the latter include:

Career Development at Goucher College, a brochure available from the Director of Admissions, Goucher College, Towson, Maryland 21204.

A Guide to Undergraduate Majors and Careers at the State University of New York at Buffalo, a handbook available from the Office of Admissions and Records, SUNY-Buffalo, 3435 Main Street, Buffalo, New York 14214.

Internships:

Further information on the internship program described in the chapter by Green, Klug, Neider, and Salem in this volume may be obtained by writing Salem at the Department of Sociology, University of Wisconsin-Whitewater, WI 53190. For details on a program that combines an internship with a career development course, write: Professor Debra Grossman, Center for the Humanities, University of Southern California, Doheny Library, Room 303, Los Angeles, CA 90007.

Establishing Closer Working Relations with Employers

1. Further details on the Community Advisory Council described by Parins in this volume may be obtained by writing him at the Department of English, University of Arkansas-Little Rock, 33rd and University, Little Rock, Arkansas 72204.

2. The games described in Honicky's chapter in this volume can be obtained at most local Bell System offices or by writing: Ms. Rita Di Martino, District Manager-Educational Relations, American Telephone and Telegraph, 195 Broadway, Rm. 532-A, New York, New York 10007.

Charles S. Green III is professor of sociology at the University of Wisconsin-Whitewater.

Richard Salem is associate professor of sociology at the University of Wisconsin-Whitewater.

Index

New Directions Quarterly Sourcebooks

New Directions for Teaching and Learning is one of several distinct series of quarterly sourcebooks published by Jossey-Bass. The sourcebooks in each series are designed to serve both as *convenient compendiums* of the latest knowledge and practical experience on their topics and as *long-life reference tools.*

One-year, four-sourcebook subscriptions for each series cost $18 for individuals (when paid by personal check) and $30 for institutions, libraries, and agencies. Single copies of earlier sourcebooks are available at $6.95 each *prepaid* (or $7.95 each when *billed*).

A complete listing is given below of current and past sourcebooks in the *New Directions for Teaching and Learning* series. The titles and editors-in-chief of the other series are also listed. To subscribe, or to receive further information, write: New Directions Subscriptions, Jossey-Bass Inc., Publishers, 433 California Street, San Francisco, California 94104.

New Directions for Teaching and Learning
Kenneth E. Eble and John F. Noonan, Editors-in-Chief
1980:   1. *Improving Teaching Styles,* Kenneth E. Eble
        2. *Learning, Cognition, and College Teaching,*
           Wilbert J. McKeachie
        3. *Fostering Critical Thinking,* Robert E. Young
        4. *Learning About Teaching,* John F. Noonan
1981:   5. *The Administrator's Role in Effective Teaching,* Alan E. Guskin

New Directions for Child Development
William Damon, Editor-in-Chief

New Directions for College Learning Assistance
Kurt V. Lauridsen, Editor-in-Chief

New Directions for Community Colleges
Arthur M. Cohen, Editor-in-Chief
Florence B. Brawer, Associate Editor

New Directions for Continuing Education
Alan B. Knox, Editor-in-Chief

New Directions for Exceptional Children
James J. Gallagher, Editor-in-Chief